ORIENTAL INSTITUTE COMMUNICATIONS • No. 25

THE ORIENTAL INSTITUTE OF THE UNIVERSITY OF CHICAGO

Thomas A. Holland, Editor
with the Assistance of Thomas G. Urban

FIGURINES AND OTHER CLAY OBJECTS FROM SARAB AND CAYÖNÜ

Vivian Broman Morales

with Preface by

R. J. Braidwood

THE ORIENTAL INSTITUTE OF THE UNIVERSITY OF CHICAGO

ORIENTAL INSTITUTE COMMUNICATIONS • No. 25

CHICAGO • ILLINOIS

Library of Congress Catalog Card Number: 89-63967

ISBN: 0-918986-59-1
ISSN: 0146-678X

The Oriental Institute, Chicago

Dedicated to

Linda S. and Robert J. Braidwood

TABLE OF CONTENTS

LIST OF PLATES

LIST OF CATALOGS

PREFACE

R. J. Braidwood

There are two brief general descriptions of the University of Chicago Oriental Institute's Prehistoric Project's field activities and research goals published since its inception in 1947 (R. J. Braidwood 1972, 1986).

After three field seasons in the Iraqi Zagros, the Project's activities there were intercepted by political events. In 1959-60, the Project undertook a field season in the region about Kermanshah in the Iranian Zagros. The season's field work was done cooperatively with our old student and friend, Dr. Ezat O. Negahban, then of the Iranian Government's Antiquities Service.

The Iranian field year began with a general surface survey of sites in the Kermanshah valley plain and its dependencies. Subsequently, modest test excavations were undertaken in several rock shelters and also on four open sites. One of these was a small mound called Sarab.

SARAB

The mound had already been pitted by nearby villagers and the eroding edges of the pits provided a generous sample of potsherds. Many of the sherds were of types already familiar to us from pottery we had recovered in portions of the upper layers of Jarmo in the Iraqi Zagros (Adams 1983). We thus decided to make a few clearances in the undisturbed portions of Sarab (R. J. Braidwood 1960a, 1960b, 1961, 1968; Braidwood, Howe, and Reed 1961).

By late 1962, it had become clear that several different younger colleagues, American, Canadian, and Danish, were assuming research efforts in southwestern Iran. At the same time it had finally developed that the Oriental Institute's Prehistoric Project could anticipate forming a joint field program with the Prehistory Section of Istanbul University. The purpose was to undertake field research along the southeastern Tauros piedmont, an area that had attracted our interest for some time.

Given this opportunity of work in southeastern Turkey, we arranged with our colleagues in the Western Asiatic section of the Royal Ontario Museum in Toronto for them to take over our excavation records and the share of the Sarab antiquities allowed us by the Antiquities Service. The Sarab artifacts were to complement the yield from the difficult-to-expose basal layers of the large mound of Godin Tepe, which was being excavated at the time by our Canadian colleague, T. Cuyler Young, Jr. Only the Sarab figurine category was held over in Chicago for the preparation of the present report by Vivian Broman Morales, who had already reported on the Jarmo figurines (Broman Morales 1983).

The Sarab site itself was subsequently examined and further tested by the Toronto colleagues as part of a survey of their own in the Kermanshah region (Levine 1976; Levine and McDonald 1977). The materials that the Toronto colleagues collected at Sarab, along with those of the earlier

Prehistoric Project lot already in the Royal Ontario Museum, were utilized in the preparation of a doctoral dissertation and in a separate study (McDonald 1979; Henrickson and McDonald 1983).

We agree with McDonald's observations (see p. 1f.) that there was a degree of difference in the nature of the Sarab deposits in Operation I and Operation V (our other exposures were very small in area), and that the artifactual yield from Operation I (abbreviated "SI", plus a level number, in catalog 1) showed a high degree of consistency.

For more detailed understandings of Sarab, more excavation would certainly be necessary. Unfortunately, the present political circumstances have prevented Toronto's further field work in the whole region.

We do feel confident that the Sarab assemblage of Operation I ("SI") reflects an advanced aspect of that seen at Jarmo. We also thoroughly agree with Mortensen's (1964) feeling that the prehistoric horizon at nearby Tepe Guran is also part of the same general assemblage, although we do wonder whether the few pertinent radiocarbon age assays for all three sites may not reflect too late a time span. Hole (1987) has recently given judicious thought to chronological matters for the Zagros region. If Sarab is to be dated just after 6000 B.C. (Libby, uncalibrated), but Çayönü's assays range around twelve hundred years earlier for an artifactual assemblage with some important linkages to those of the above three (Guran, Jarmo, and Sarab), we still have much to learn about the pace of early-village developments along the Zagros flanks.

ÇAYÖNÜ

From its start, the Joint Istanbul-Chicago Universities' Prehistoric Project was under the co-directorship of Prof. Dr. Halet Çambel and Robert J. Braidwood. For each season, the junior field staff was largely made up of Çambel's advanced students, but there were also a succession of foreign students. In 1978, Prof. Dr. Wulf Schirmer, head of the Institut für Baugeschichte of Karlsruhe University, his assistant Werner Schnuchel, and again a succession of Schirmer's students joined the Çayönü field team. In 1986, Doc. Dr. Mehmet Özdogan of Istanbul's Prehistory Section was advanced to the active directorship of the Prehistoric Project. Given the official regulation that excavated antiquities may not be exported from Turkey, it was particularly fortunate for us that Broman Morales was able to participate in two different field seasons at Çayönü and to examine the Çayönü figurines both in the Diyarbakir Museum and those temporarily in the Prehistory Section in Istanbul.

In the early autumn of 1963, the Prehistoric Project began surface surveys in the vilayet of Siirt, moved presently to the northern part of the Diyarbakir vilayet, and spent a short time in the northwestern portion of the Urfa vilayet (Çambel and Braidwood 1980). The site with the most promising surface yield, for our particular interest, was a low mound of ca. 50,000 m squared area called Çayönü Tepesi. It lies in a valley plain of modest size at the foot of a main ridge of the eastern Tauros mountains, in the uppermost Tigris river drainage, near a town called Ergani.

By the autumn of 1988, we had completed our thirteenth field season at Çayönü and had exposed approximately 5000 m squared area of the main early village-farming community horizon. At this writing, there are some twenty-five well-clustered radiocarbon age assays, ca. 7400 to 6850 B.C. (Libby, uncalibrated), for Çayönü's main prehistoric phase. The site is especially remarkable in its yield of architectural information (Schirmer 1983, 1988), but remarkable also as regards its variety of burial habits (Özbek 1988) and the presence of small but numerous copper artifacts (Stech, in press).

Although much more evidence has been acquired since our last general account (Çambel and Braidwood 1983), we are still far from able to present a crisp and clear explanation of all that went on during the main prehistoric phase at Çayönü. We do feel sure that the general Çayönü assemblage leans more clearly towards the yields from the Zagros and northern Iraqi sites, than to those now available from the restricted salvage exposures along the mid-upper Euphrates and towards the Levant. There are architectural details, a characteristic type of obsidian blade, various ground stone objects, and a few of the clay figurine types that Broman Morales discusses below as cases in point.

The matter of restricted versus broad exposures requires a further comment regarding Çayönü and Broman Morales' report on the site's figurines. On sites with only a restricted exposure a stratigraphic sequence may well have an apparent layer cake-like horizontality—hence "levels" may appear to be very well behaved. However, for excavations with broad exposures such as we have made over our thirteen field seasons at Çayönü, it soon becomes readily apparent that a strict horizontality of levels is not necessarily the rule. We now know there were at least five successive "domestic" building plan types. In our last general account (Çambel and Braidwood 1983) we were sure of a succession of only three types of "domestic" plans. This situation leaves us with the still unfinished task of doing our best to assign exact sequential order to each individual findspot.

Thus Broman Morales' listings of findspots (catalog 2) for the illustrated figurines reflect this unfinished task. All we can say with finality at the moment is that all of the figurines she considers here are, with very few exceptions, part of the main prehistoric phase assemblage.

***

One final remark pertains to both the collections of figurines presented here. Far less exposure was made at Sarab than at Çayönü, but the sheer quantity of examples recovered is exactly opposite. We have never experienced so light and almost fluffy a matrix as was that of Sarab—it was remarkably easy to recover artifacts there. At Çayönü, on the other hand, the matrix was a tough hard clay (literally a gumbo when wet) making the recognition and clearance of clay figurines very difficult. However, we do not feel that this is the only reason for the paucity of clay figurines at Çayönü, rather, it seems that figurine manufacture was simply not given as much importance as was the case along the Zagros.

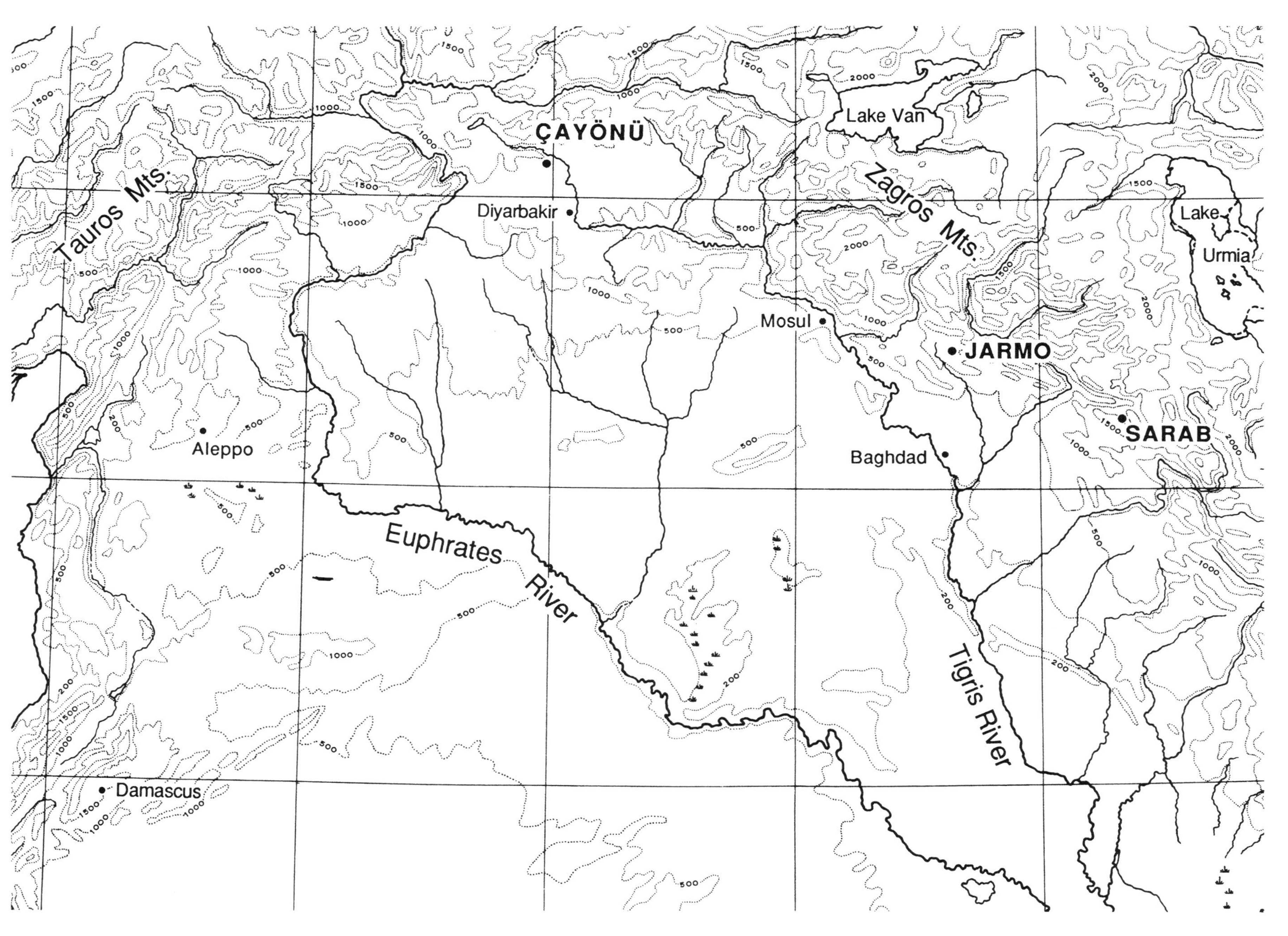

Map Showing Locations of Jarmo in Iraq, Sarab in Iran, and Çayönü in Turkey

FIGURINES AND OTHER CLAY OBJECTS FROM SARAB

INTRODUCTION AND GENERAL DISCUSSION

Tepe Sarab is a low mound to the east of the town of Kermanshah. The Kermanshah valley is broad with cultivable land, water, and wild game, which make it an attractive area for early village settlement. Abundant water is available from the nearby Qara Su; a spring also is located immediately to the north.

All of the archaeological investigations of this site by the Oriental Institute's Iranian Prehistoric Project took place in the early months of 1960 (R. J. Braidwood 1972; Braidwood, Howe, and Reed 1961). Two main areas were excavated from March to May, Operations I and V. As the field season was short and the area uncovered was small (estimated as less than 10% of the whole site), the material evidence is relatively scant. This is due in part also to the intrusion of later pits all through the area investigated. Another factor, however, aided enormously in the recovery of small objects, especially the clay figurines: the fluffiness of the soil bedded with ash layers. Approximately 2,400 shaped clay pieces were recovered, a remarkable amount for the small area excavated. This collection is discussed in this paper.

Clay figurines were found in great numbers deep in level SIc, 2a toward the west end of the central trench in Operation I. In general, the lowest levels of this operation had abundant clay figurine material and snail shells, while potsherds were scarce. McDonald (1979) describes Operation I as containing a cluster of six or seven shallow pit houses, which suggest to her that the community consisted of between twelve and twenty inhabitants.

The small size of these pits (4-6 m in diameter in oval form), in turn, led McDonald to suggest habitation by single individuals—rather than family groups—who used Sarab as a seasonal site. She speculates that the occupants may have been largely a group of males using the site as a base for hunting, or for the knapping of flint which occurs in outcrops nearby. However, Bökönyi (1977:37) believes that there was year-round occupation at Sarab.

I would also question McDonald's view because of the number and variety of clay figurines found, especially in the lowest levels. If my theory is correct that these were individual magic wish-figures, the diversification of forms would indicate occupation by a family group or groups, even if that occupation were seasonal over a period of several hundred years. McDonald also notes that, since similar undulating layered deposits exist throughout the levels excavated, some continuity in pattern for the pit house structures seems likely.

Another consideration brought out in McDonald's dissertation is that Operation V shows a completely different stratigraphy from that of Operation I. The undulating ashy layers are not present here. In reviewing the cultural remains and the absence of what could be interpreted as architectural features, McDonald suggests that this area was an outside area in the sense that not only was it not used during the occupation span of the area of Operation I, but also that it was outside of the houses occupied by the Sarab inhabitants at a later period than that of Operation I. This is deduced by the difference in the artifactual materials, since Operation V contained what could have been produced and used outside of a house in a yard or patio context. The clay figurine material is indeed notably sparse in this area, even though the excavation went to 1.5 m to 2 m in depth, and gives no chronological clue. Fragments of figurines were found at the lowest level (level 5), but throughout Operation V the clay material was mostly in the form of miscellaneous shaped pieces.

The soil in Operation V was quite consolidated, which meant less favorable preservation, and hence recovery, of the lightly baked clay bits. Excavation, however, was done very carefully here in order to pick up any traces of architecture, such as post-holes, and therefore not much artifactual material could have been overlooked. In addition, since figurine material had been so abundant in the ashy layers of Operation I, careful watch was kept for shaped clay while screening the excavated soil from Operation V.

Thus, as far as the category of clay figurines is concerned, McDonald's interpretation of Operation V as an area outside of Operation I habitation seems valid. The distribution record for the clay figurine material shows that the major categories are indeed represented in Operation V, though the total number is very small. There is a proportionally larger amount of unclassifiable clay material from Operation V than from Operation I, but this is readily explained if Operation V were outside of the occupation areas, where identifiable fragments were found in great numbers.

As at Jarmo, great concentrations of snail shells were found (Braidwood 1983:542f.) especially in the lower levels. This land snail (*Helix salomonica*) was gathered for food and undoubtedly was the inspiration for the abstract form of female figurine, here called "snail lady." I prefer to think that the Sarab figurine makers saw the snail shell as an attractive form to copy rather than that it suggested to them a mystical female-snail affinity.

In the discussion of the human figurines, it is demonstrated how the abstract forms evolve from, or take the place of, the more realistic composite forms.

The human figurine category is the largest of the divisions of classifiable clay material. This is due in part to the inclusion of three types of abstract forms that I consider as representing the human female. Next in size is the animal figurine category with three identifiable types—dog, pig, and horned animal (sheep/goat)—and three other types, not identifiable, of small animals.

Two other important categories are those of abstract forms, for which it is difficult, if not impossible, to assess meaning or use, and geometric forms. In the latter category, balls are the most common type, but discs, cones, tetrahedrons, and rod sections are also considered in this category.

The presence of stone objects such as beads and labret-like studs has resulted in a few imitations of these forms in clay. The perforated object category also includes pieces that resemble spindle whorls save for their small size. The asymmetry of perforation and the narrowness of the perforation itself also preclude the actual use of these items as whorls. (Only four pieces are classified as possibly being spindle whorls.)

The above five categories have been established in classifying the figurine material. Each category is discussed, described, and conclusions are drawn. In a few instances, the types are further divided into classified and questionably-classified pieces, thus minimizing the overloading of a type and allowing better comparison with other collections.

The clay figurines of the main categories are often beautifully made and show great manual dexterity on the part of their makers, since the pieces are generally quite small. Many are covered with fingerprints, while others appear to have been grass-wiped. Others are carefully smoothed or even burnished.

In addition to the above five categories, I have established a miscellaneous category to discuss the textile, mat, and basket impressions, a few varied objects, and, above all, a fair amount of shaped clay fragments.

There are textile impressions on some of the pieces; several of these show a fine simple weave (one warp and one woof thread). Mat and basket impressions occur on several clay lumps. There is some use of red ochre or an orange-red paint on figurine fragments from different categories.

The shaped clay fragments do not fit into any of the established categories but must be considered part of the collection of figurines, since there has been some shaping or modeling. It would seem that at least some of these fragments were pieces of raw material kept at hand during the modeling of whatever wish-figure was being produced at the moment. Pieces were probably pinched off or excess clay bits were added to these lumps as the work progressed.

Finally, in addition to all of the above, there is a considerable bulk of random clay fragments (in the sense of volume, over 50 cubic decimeters—only a very small fraction of the large quantities left in the Tehran Museum) which does not contain any modeled or shaped material and which I am not considering in this report. These fragments may, however, offer much of interest to those concerned with architectural clay as they contain reed, straw, and stick impressions. There could even be impressions of seeds, grains, or grasses, since some of the figurines themselves show inclusions of pebbles or pieces of shell, or impressions of sticks, straws, and grass.

In concluding this introduction, it is important to note that the general small size and fragmentary state of the majority of the figurine pieces make it very difficult to decide what the collection represents. Impermanence and short-lived expectations seem to be indicated, if the categories of animal and human figurines, at least, are indeed wish-figurines (see p. 9).

The descriptions that follow are really much better realized in the drawings. All pieces have been drawn at 1:1 scale (unless otherwise indicated) so as to facilitate the comparison of different objects.

ANIMAL FIGURINES (pls. 1-5 and 6a-c)

DISCUSSION

Animal forms are separated into types based mainly on tail position. This seems to work fairly well for the three types which can be given specific animal identification: the curly-tailed dog, the pig, and the horned animals (sheep and goats). It is difficult to distinguish between the sheep and goat figures except for a few whole examples which clearly depict a bearded goat or a woolly sheep. The horns, however, show the difference by the cross-section, round for sheep, pinched ridge for goat. Unfortunately, the horns are usually broken off and, of the separate horns recovered, very few correspond in size to the heads of this type. The sheep/goat figures generally have a short tab tail which turns up or down, never out. The pig has a short tail which extends out, while the curly-tailed dog has its tail turned up and curled over the back. Heads found separately, head and forepart fragments, and body fragments, whose tail position cannot be determined, are put in the non-classifiable type, except for those clearly recognizable as pig or sheep/goat.

While some of the figurines suggest certain animals apart from the three types mentioned above, it is not possible to ascertain just what these other animals might have been. Wild animals were certainly hunted or captured and small wild animals are surely depicted in clay, but which animals it is hard to say.

In classifying these plastic representations of animal forms, caution must be used, however, in making specific animal identification. For this reason, for example, only those figures with a curled-over tail have been identified as dogs, since no other known animal has that particular attribute.

A large portion of the animal figurines are modeled with the forelegs shaped together in an extended position, while the hind legs are done in the same fashion and give the figure a stable flat base. I first put these flat-based forms in a separate division, but, when all of the types were well established, it could be seen that all types of animals are represented here in the flat-based forms. Therefore, the animal type itself and not the posture (suggestive of that of a passive animal, alert but resting) was important to the modeler. Forming a flat base makes a more stable figure with none of the problems—to the modeler—of fitting on or pulling out four legs from the plastic clay. All of the important identifying features could be presented in an upright position with no difficulty.

The use of tail position might be considered an inadequate qualifier for typing. However, once the types were clear, tail position really did seem to be a valid criterion for the pig, dog, and horned animals. Of course, different species of animals may be represented in each type that has had to be identified by tail position alone.

CURLY-TAILED DOGS (pl. 1a-l) 33 examples

Bökönyi (1977:33-34) states that only the dog and the wild wolf/dog are present at Sarab. The wolf does not have a curly tail, so it is evident that the clay figurines at Sarab which show the tail curved up and over the back represent dogs. With the presence of domesticated sheep at that time, it seems reasonable to assume that Sarab dogs were domesticated to the point that they would not disturb the flocks. Since the hunting of wild animals still played a large part in the early village economy, the dogs must have been very useful. If not fed from the hunt, they themselves could have hunted smaller animals such as the hare and badger, and perhaps even deer and gazelle by hunting in packs.

Seventeen figurines definitely have the tail curled up over the back. Sixteen other fragments are not as clear and are therefore questionably classified as curly-tailed dogs. Of the total, four are flat-based, three of these are in the questionable division, and four have incised neck lines.

Half of these figurines are more or less whole. When present, the head is held up and there is a short muzzle which ends in a rounded tip. Of the twenty examples which have heads, only five have punctate eyes, while one has short-line incisions for eyes and an incised mouth as well (pl. 1c). The mouth is indicated by an incised line on six examples; only one of these, just mentioned, also has eyes. The ears are short and are pointed up or forward. The forelegs are extended slightly, while the hind legs are short and straight or are extended slightly back. On six examples the legs are set apart from the body by deep thumbnail incisions. One small figure has parallel vertical finger-nail incisions on both sides of the body presumably to indicate shaggy hair (pl. 1m).

Genitals may be indicated on one example by a tab of clay between the hind legs that is set apart by a deep incision on either side (pl. 1l). Three others, questionably classified, seem to have an appliquéd piece between the hind legs (pl. 1i), and one of the flat-based examples has a small, horizontally incised button appliquéd beneath the tail (pl. 1j).

All but three figurines have the pinched spine. Two of the smooth-backed ones are tiny and one of these is also flat-based. The third example is 44 mm long and is flat-based. (These two flat-based figurines are in the questionable group.)

In size these figurines range from medium (32-44 mm) to small (21 mm long). The posture generally suggests an alert animal that is ready to run.

WILD PIGS (pls. 2a-h and 6a, b) 42 examples

Bökönyi (1977:29f.) clearly claims domesticated pigs at Sarab; Flannery (1983:176) complains that the available sample is hardly large enough to be reliable.

Wild pigs could be destructive of crops under cultivation so that the killing of these animals might not always be for food. By protecting the crops, man was also protecting part of his food supply. The newly domesticated ungulates also would have to be protected from attack by predators such as the bear, leopard, wolf, and wild pig. Dogs would be useful in helping man with such protection.

The figurines which most clearly portray the wild pig are distinguished by a massive head which terminates in a long vertically-flattened snout that is accentuated by a high crest of the pinched spine behind the ears and a body with the pinched spine that tapers straight back to a short tail which either extends out or is turned down. The tails on all of the examples classified as pigs have broken off completely or are very short.

Domestication of the pig seems to be a moot point at Sarab. The wild pig in the Zagros was and still is smaller than the Central European wild pig (Bökönyi 1977:29). A striking effect of domestication is the smaller size of the domesticates and, in the pig, a shortening of the snout. I would consider that, because of the long snout, the clay animal figurines categorized as pigs would represent the wild rather than the domesticated animal.

Only two figurines, both in the Tehran Museum (not illustrated here), have incised necks with a double line on each side of the head. These two also have small punctate eyes and incised mouth; one also has ear punctates. One other figure, whose nose has been broken away, seems to have had punctated ears as well as eyes. In addition it has three punctations on the under part of the body, two on the right side and one between the front legs.

One of the best examples of what must be a boar has a big head with a long snout and a short tapered body (pls. 2a and 6a). The mouth is incised and has a deep perforation on the right side, perhaps for the insertion of a straw to suggest a tusk. The perforation is 10 mm deep. A deep gash under the left side of the lower jaw makes it difficult to ascertain whether there was a perforation here for the other tusk, but this is probable. The tail is short and rounded down. Genitals may be indicated by deep nail incisions on both sides of a tab of clay under the tail and between the legs. The legs are short, extended slightly, and are set apart from the body by deep thumb-nail incisions. There are three holes on the right side of the body and the left side is criss-crossed by incised lines. These body lines were first finely incised horizontally. Then the vertical lines were cut down through these and deeply scored the plastic clay. This figure would apparently indicate an animal desired in the hunt, the wild boar.

Another example, carelessly made and pressed down flat while still plastic, seems to have been a similar boar figure (pl. 6b). The head is massive, the nose was bent down at the tip when the misshaping happened, the rounded back tapers to a small tab tail, and the legs, originally extended like the previous example, are flattened up toward the body as though the figure was set up while still plastic and doubled up under the weight. These two figures measure 57 mm and 64 mm long respectively.

A smaller example (pl. 2b), 37 mm long and very nicely modeled, has the underside of the snout broken away. The head is narrow with a pinched top and short ears up close to the crest. The spine is pinched high and scored with parallel fingernail incisions down to a short tail which has broken off. The forelegs and hind legs are extended and seem to indicate a running animal.

Genitals may be represented on four examples, three of which are questionably classified. Two such genital representations are in the form of a vertically incised appliquéd button which has been partially broken away, and one (pl. 2d) is a tab of clay set off by incisions. One of the small, questionably classified figurines has an incised mouth, punctate eyes and ears, and is covered over both sides of the body with very fine-line short gashes and semi-circular punctates (pl. 2e).

There are nine examples which consist of the head only. One large very well-modeled piece has a vertically pinched snout with two small vertical gashes where tusks would be (pl. 2h). Neither mouth nor eyes are detailed, but the short upright ears are punctated. There is a deep single-line incision that demarks the jawline, and the high thin crest has parallel-line fingernail incisions down both sides. Another smaller head, which is questionably classified, has an incised mouth, no eyes, and parallel fingernail incisions down both sides. An even smaller head has punctate eyes and an incised mouth.

Twenty of the figurines of this type have heads, but only six have punctate eyes and incised mouths. Four of the questionably classified fragments have heads. Of these, two have punctate eyes and incised mouths. Of the forty-two figurines in this group, eight are questionably classified and eight are heads only.

HORNED ANIMALS (pl. 3a-m) 255 examples

It can be assumed that wild sheep and goat were first hunted along with the red deer, bones of which were found in great numbers at Asiab, an earlier site in the Kermanshah Valley (Bökönyi 1977:27). The presence of wild goats in any area leads to rapid deforestation so that the red deer, which inhabited only large dense forests, soon disappeared. By Sarab settlement times there were no longer any red deer to be hunted and gazelle had taken over the resulting dry steppe environment. It is difficult to determine from bone fragments whether or not a sheep or a goat is domesticated. However, there must have been wild sheep and goats still in the area to be hunted along with the wild pig and the gazelle.

The study of the animal bones of Sarab by Bökönyi indicates that animal husbandry was well established with sheep and goats but no cattle. In discussing the productivity of animal domestication as opposed to hunting, Bökönyi points out that not all hunting-gathering groups eventually took up animal husbandry. He suggests that those who did acted under pressure from growing populations and were thus forced to insure a stable supply of food near settled dwellings. The competition for wild animals by hunting parties could no longer guarantee food for all. At Sarab hunting was still of about equal importance to domestic flocks, as shown by the large numbers of gazelle bones that were found in the excavations.

For the figurines, the sheep/goat type is established by various characteristics, the most important of which is the presence of horns or rather the evidence of horns that have broken off, as is the case with the majority of these figures. The head and forepart are the most diagnostic, but there are also body characteristics that suggest sheep/goat even without the head. These include a fold or frontal projection between the forelegs which possibly represents hair, a smooth flat back that broadens at the rear, and often a broad fold between the hind legs. Where this fold exists, the legs are quite rudimentary and are sometimes merely folded under (pl. 3g). The tail is short and is up or down, never out. According to Schaller (1980), who has observed modern wild goats and wild sheep, the wild goat in rut carries its tail straight up. Goats also have beards and tails that are long, flat, and bare underneath; sheep have round rat-like tails.

This animal figurine type has been titled "horned animals," since it is seldom possible to distinguish the sheep from the goats in the figurine forms. Nor has it been possible to identify any figure as representing gazelle or deer, although the animal bone study shows the presence of both of these animals.

One of the figurines that can be identified as a goat has a beard (pl. 3a). The horns and short upturned tail are broken off. There is a fold between the outstretched front legs and a partially broken off fold between the short straight hind legs. A fragmentary sheep figurine shows wool by the chevron incising along its sides (pl. 3b). This figurine is cited by Bökönyi (1977:25 and fig. 17) who points out that only the domestic sheep have curly wool which has long fibers. This in turn explains to Bökönyi why the majority of sheep were kept to adult age and not killed while young when the best meat could have been obtained.

Generally the examples in this division do not seem to be well modeled, but this may seem so because of their battered and fragmentary state. From one head fragment with part of the horn remaining (pl. 3j) one can see that, as whole figures, they were really quite realistic.

The total number of examples of this type is 255. Of these, forty-six are more or less whole and six of them flat-based. There are twenty-two head and forepart fragments, one of which is flat-based, and fifty-six body fragments, seventeen flat-based. There are also eighteen flat-based figures that are questionably classified; four are more or less whole, one is a forepart with head, and thirteen are body fragments only. In addition, there are nineteen heads and ninety-four horns (64 goat, 30 sheep; two of the goat horns show traces of red paint).

Horns are classified by section and those with round sections represent sheep (pl. 3h, m). There are thirty of these, sixteen with rounded or pointed tips and fourteen with the tips broken off. Those with a pinched or keeled edge represent goats (pl. 3i-l), sixty-four in total, of which fifteen have tips, twenty-three have the tips broken off, and there are an additional twenty-six short pieces (mid-section fragments).

ANIMALS WITH TAIL UP (pl. 4a-c) 61 examples

The figurines in this group are medium to small in size. (Some that I originally classified here were transferred to the dog type as questionably classified.) There are now twenty-five examples which are more or less whole and twenty-five fragments that show little but tail position (including two fragments of tails only). The tail can be straight up or angled out from the body. These figures probably represent a small animal, possibly a dog. Thirty-eight of the total have the pinched spine. One has double line neck incisions and four have single line incisions. Half of the type is flat-based; eight of these are more or less whole with the pinched spine. One also has neck incisions and three are fragments. Two more or less whole figures and eleven fragments have smooth backs. Two examples have punctate eyes (pl. 4b, c). In addition, there are eleven fragments of back ends.

ANIMALS WITH TAIL OUT (pl. 4d-k) 92 examples

The figurines in this group are medium to small in size, some of which are the best modeled figures in the animal category. The tail is always broken off but was large, round in section, and projected straight out behind the body; all of which suggest a bushy tail. The head is usually positioned up and forward and the legs are extended and often modeled together to form a flat base; more than half of the examples of this type are so based. Fourteen of the more or less whole figures, only two of which are flat-based, have punctate eyes; nine of these also have an incised mouth.

Here the flat base can be seen as a method of manufacture rather than as a characteristic animal posture. A small running figure is more easily modeled with the legs together so as to provide a stable base; at the same time the impression of movement is not lost.

Again, the size of these figurines suggests a small animal; the posture and alertness suggest a wild and therefore hunted form. Of the more or less whole figures, a total of fifty-two examples, thirty-six have the flat base. There are also forty fragmentary figurines, and twenty-two with the flat base.

ANIMALS WITH TAIL DOWN (pl. 4l-o) 29 examples

In this group the animal represented again seems to be a small one as the size range is from medium to small. A few larger fragments (more than half of the figurines of this type are fragmentary) could have represented pigs, but without the head it is not possible to designate them as such. One almost whole figure has a long tail (pl. 4l). With head held high, ears pricked up, and legs extended, this figure suggests a lively animal, perhaps a fox. In general, when the head has not been broken off, it is held high and on five out of the thirteen whole examples the mouth is incised. Three also have punctate eyes. The back tends to be smooth. Few of these figurines have the flat base.

NON-CLASSIFIABLE ANIMAL FIGURINES (pls. 5a-q and 6c) 258 examples

Foreparts, with or without heads, or fragments whose tail position cannot be determined make up this group. Examples consisting only of heads also are considered here; there are twenty-seven of these. Five fragments of foreparts show the incised neck (pl. 5b, c) while about seventy have the flat base.

One small figure with extended forelegs has gashed punctates for eyes and ears (pl. 5a). Another small figure has pin prick punctates covering the neck and spine (pl. 5d).

A tiny flat-based forepart with head has a double row of pin prick punctates down the back (pl. 5e). There is also a gashed perforation between the rows which goes through to the base. This fragment also has an incised mouth and punctate eyes. The rest of this unclassifiable material is too fragmentary to permit further description. Seventy-two small fragments are classified as legs.

The twenty-seven heads can be divided into four types. Type A belongs to a small animal; it is nicely modeled and has an incised mouth (pl. 5f, g). It could easily belong to the group of animals with the tail out or to the curly-tailed dogs. There are thirteen examples. Type B has a very pointed nose; there are five of these (pl. 5h, i). Type C has a short head with rounded nose; five examples are placed here (pl. 5j, k). Type D is badly battered and the nose is broken off, so identification is difficult; there are only four of these.

Finally, there a few figurines of special interest. One of these is a double-headed form (pl. 6c). Both ends show a face with punctates for eyes and, on one end only, a single punctate for the mouth. This end is rounded on top and the "face" is formed by a vertical pinching all the way to the base. The other head is squarish with "ears" and a pinch to form the face. The base is flattened and arched with the ends rounded. Both sides of this piece are covered with short-line gashed incisions in vertical parallel lines.

Another has a big round head with little or no nose and a wide grin that is incised under two widely spaced punctate eyes, all of which form what looks like a human face. The short forelegs are extended; the back seems smooth and rounded. (These last two figurines are in the Tehran Museum but were not available to me in May, 1978. I am basing these descriptions on field photographs.)

Other figurines of note are the squashed and twisted forms, some of which have been described in their type group. There is one in the tail out type that is unusual for its round head and appliquéd pellet eyes (pl. 5m). The nose and mouth seem to have been added by applying bits of clay rather than modeling the features. With such apparent care in the manufacture of this piece it seems strange that the maker should have then distorted it; it was not squashed while drying but deformed in the making. Other examples, including one large figurine that was squeezed in the fist of its modeler (pl. 5o), show the bizarre forms that may result and make classification impossible (pl. 5l-q).

This misshaping, squashing, or twisting gives the impression that the figure itself was not important, that it was the act of giving the clay form that was the reason for the manufacture. Another clue is, of course, the fragmentary and battered state of most of the animal material. The general small size of the pieces is also noteworthy. The makers did not seem to be concerned with creating anything like a small statue or votive object to be preserved and venerated.

These little figures required a great deal of manual dexterity and some skill to produce. Therefore there must have been an important stimulus for their creation.

There is no way of distinguishing figurines made by the same individual, though fingerprints on the surface of the clay objects are quite common. With such variation in form and skill demonstrated in the clay figurine collection, it would seem likely that each person made his own wish figures.

CONCLUSIONS

Now we can speculate as to why animal figurines were made at all. The horned animal figures could be considered magic wish objects that, while they were formed in the plastic clay, "wished" for the animal to be procured by hunting. The wild sheep and wild goat still existed in the area during the time of Sarab's occupation and must have been a prime source of meat, wool, leather, bone, and horn. Although Bökönyi (1977:16-25) confirms the domestication of the sheep and the goat, he asserts that at Sarab hunting was equal in importance to animal husbandry. The evidence of the dog in the samples of animal bone and the certain identification of the curly-tailed dog in the figurine material lends color to the hunting aspect of this early village economy.

The clay figures of the pig represent a wild form. Some of these figurines show marks of piercing or cutting, which perhaps indicate the hunter's modeling of his desire to kill or otherwise secure the animal.

Many of the animal heads show punctate or slit eyes and incised or gashed mouths. In very few instances the ears are also pierced by punctates. This could perhaps be seen as the desire of the maker that the animal be clearly identified; with the ears pierced it might even be able to "hear" the wish magic. Some of the flat-based animals have the eyes and mouth indicated. In this case, the legs are not realistically presented but the head is. The male of the species appears to have been especially desirable, since a number of figurines of various types seem to have the genitals depicted.

Therefore it can be assumed that the maker knew exactly what animal he was modeling (wishing for), certainly in the case of the wild forms. There could have been a more generalized depiction in the modeling of the domestic animals (sheep, goat, and dog), since the wishes concerning them were probably of a different kind.

The variation in the shaping of all of the figurines, in every category, indicates that their manufacture was done by individuals for their own personal desires or wishes. The fact that some of these figurines were allowed to slump or twist, with legs pinched off or bent under while still plastic, shows that the wish magic was indeed in the forming of the clay; what happened to it afterward depended on the whim of the modeler. Those who did nice modeling probably set their figures carefully aside to dry, as they were pleased with the appearance of their work.

It seems certain that most of the clay material studied in this report was lightly baked in an open fire. It is logical to suppose that this firing took place in the household hearth. There is as yet no evidence for either a special firing technique or a specific place for firing, or for any shrine, household or public, where these figurines were kept in concentration. The fragmentary condition of the majority of the animal figurines also argues for a short-term "usefulness," perhaps until the wish was or was not fulfilled. Then the figurines would have been discarded and would have become mixed with the household debris in a casual and careless way, which thus caused the fragmentary condition and battered aspect of these little figures.

HUMAN FIGURINES (Pls. 6d-g and 7-14)

DISCUSSION

At Sarab the human figurine fragments are classified into seven types, all but two are designated as female. The male form is represented by eighteen fragments out of a total of 650. This makes speculation about the meaning of the male form rather difficult. It certainly would seem that this form was unimportant in view of the paucity of examples and the small size of these figurines.

Some of the human figurine forms are shown as seated; some others (torsos) are shown in erect posture and have a flat round base. These could be interpreted as representing standing figures, since it is difficult to balance a top-heavy form (this type has outstretched arms) on separately modeled legs. Modeling the figure as seated is another solution and all the other types of female figurines are seated.

Three examples of a simple extended form which is neither male nor female probably were meant to lie on their backs. They certainly do not balance on their short stubby legs. The only possible interpretation is that they represent babies.

The female figurine types are variously represented by a simple seated form, by a torso with small appliquéd breasts and arms outstretched to the sides, by a composite form built up of separately modeled parts, and by two varieties of an abstract form. Heads are generally non-realistic. There is one example of a separate head with features, one with hair but no features, and another which is a questionably classified fragment for a total of only three realistic heads.

The non-realistic heads seem to have broken off from the more realistic composite forms as well as from the two abstract varieties. Realistic features could have been considered unnecessary; the maker would probably feel that the maker's own identity was incorporated in the manufacture.

The composite form consists of a pair of legs, often tenoned together with a small stick or reed, a mid-section built up around a cone-shaped piece of clay that forms a stomach which overlapped the legs in front, and buttocks which round down over the legs in back. A stalk serves for the head and neck, which are sometimes pulled up from the mid-section mass or shaped separately and pushed down into place. Breasts, small or large and pendulous, were appliquéd to the body and overlap the stomach. Often an appliquéd strip was added as a "g-string" to the otherwise naked figure. Sometimes the legs would be decorated with punctates or short-line incisions on the top or sides. A vertical incision on both sides of the leg was sometimes used to indicate a bent knee. The whole represented a pregnant female.

The size range for this type is great; a pair of crude and battered legs with matching stick holes has a broken length of 88 mm, while other fragments are small and very well modeled. Due to the manner of manufacture this type is represented by all of the various parts, few of which we were able to reassemble to recreate the original figure.

The various abstract forms occur in the same levels throughout the site as does the composite form. Indeed, the "lady stalk" form can easily be seen as an abstraction of the composite form. The figure is simplified by using one leg to represent two and by pulling the stalk body up from the rounded back. The resulting figure is not obviously pregnant; it also lacks breasts and is otherwise not realistically modeled. Another form has a boxy leg, rather pillow-like, with two of the corners serving as feet. This form sometimes has breasts appliquéd and could represent a pregnant figure.

"Snail ladies" are an even further abstraction of the human form. The most common example takes the lady stalk leg and coils the stalk part around, clockwise or counter clockwise, to form a snail-like shape. The stalk head is still preserved on one example (pl. 6e), which makes it the key piece for this type. Many of these snail-like figures are decorated with punctates, nail incisions, line incisions, and combinations of these. This elaborate decoration suggests clothing or some sort of covering; it is conceivable that loose trousers are depicted. A variation of this type is a coil; one end serves as the leg, while the other end bends back over this leg to form the knee of the other leg. The stalk or coil then turns up to form the body and the head. This type is plain surfaced; one example has appliquéd breasts and may represent a pregnant female.

There are finally a few miscellaneous figurines that, while representing the female figure, are not classifiable into any of the above types. Most seem to be variations of the lady stalk (an abstract form), each of which is described separately.

SIMPLE EXTENDED FORMS (pl. 7a, b) 3 examples

There are only three figurines in this category. One is whole with a round flattened face on which eyes are punctated and a smiling mouth is incised (pl. 7a). There is no modeling of the head which joins the body directly; the figure, which possesses short stumpy legs, does not stand. The smooth, slightly rounded back shows that this figure was meant to lie flat. There are no sexual characteristics by which to classify it, so it is assumed that this piece depicts a baby.

The other two figurines are less realistic, one has a blunt-ended stump head (pl. 7b) and the other is more battered and fragmentary. They are all about the same size (42-44 mm long). It is most interesting to find what seems to be the form of a baby depicted alone. In later times, female figurines are wide-hipped, big-breasted, and sometimes hold a baby or child. (At Sarab wide-hipped female figurines with large pendulous breasts are present, but they usually lack arms and never have a baby figure associated with them.) These three simple forms seem out of scale with the majority of the composite type of female figure. They are too large and too crudely modeled to go with the nicely modeled parts that make up the realistic female figurines. There is a possibility that in the case of these three examples a mother could have fashioned the piece for her daughter to play with.

SIMPLE SEATED FORMS (pl. 7c-h) 17 examples

The size range for this form is considerable, from medium-small to tiny. This figurine type is made all in one piece; the basic shape is that of an equilateral triangle with the basal corners bent forward to form the legs and with the apex serving for the stalk head (pl. 7h). The result can be fairly realistic, as in one example with appliquéd arms, seated cross-legged (pl. 7c), or very abstract as in the tiny form with a pointed stalk head (pl. 7d). Aside from the example with appliquéd arms, the figurines, unlike the extended-arm type, do not have any appendages, either arms or breasts.

One figure has nicely shaped legs which suggest a bent-knee seated position (pl. 7e). Unfortunately, the body is broken off at the waist. The possibility exists that the upper part could have had extended arms. Six additional legs are included here because of their resemblance to this bent-knee example. (In the composite and abstract types, the legs are extended or bent to the side.) In another fragment, a piece of clay folded horizontally gives the figure, which is broken at the waist, a stomach fold over two short legs divided vertically (pl. 7f). The leg division extends to the back and thus delineates the buttocks. A long deep gash across the stomach may represent the umbilicus. This fragment does not sit well; the body tilts back and leaves the legs in the air. The figure is quite crude but, since it appears to be wide-hipped, it is classified as female.

Only one figurine shows any decoration (pl. 7g). Again the body is broken off at the waist and the back is sheared off. The decoration consists of two parallel lines of nail incisions on the top of the left leg. Several incisions can be seen on the right leg where it is broken off close to the body.

In conclusion, this form is simple, poorly defined, often crudely modeled, and very fragmentary. The tiny example (pl. 7d) is the only whole figurine in this group of seventeen examples and is quite abstract.

TORSOS WITH EXTENDED ARMS—MALE (pl. 7i-o) 18 examples

The only human figurines that could be considered male are of this type. Not only are these fragments small, but they are also rather crudely modeled. The bodies may be flat-based torsos or they may be seated with short legs pulled out of the body clay as illustrated on plate 7k-n. Two of these seated figures (pl. 7k, m) seem to have a back rest to balance the form, since the outstretched arms make it top-heavy. The arms of this type are not only outstretched but rounded forward as if in an open embrace. The shoulders are often quite massive and the back is rounded. A head of some sort, either a rounded stump or a pinched face, was made for this type. Only one (pl. 7i) seems to have a spade beard pinched out horizontally. A total of five fragments have heads, three of which are stumps only, while two are pinched vertically (pl. 7j, o). One of these has punctate eyes.

For the male form it would seem that a head of some sort was considered necessary, but the most important aspect is that of the all-embracing posture of the arms. Could this mean social power in the form of leadership? If generative power is supposed to be indicated, it is in a totally abstract form.

There are only eighteen examples in this group, one of which is in the laboratory of the Tehran Museum. Against the overwhelming number and variety of shapes for the female figurine it is obvious that wish-magic concerning the human male was not very important, whatever aspect it may have had.

TORSOS WITH EXTENDED ARMS—FEMALE (pl. 8a-i) 15 examples

This type is distinguished from the male form in three ways: wide hips, stump arms outstretched to the sides, and small appliquéd breasts. Generally, these fragments are small and better modeled than the male form. All have had heads which are broken off. The arms are stumpy and extend out to the sides at shoulder level, rather than curving inward in an embracing position.

One figurine has parallel incised lines on the back and sides (pl. 8f), another is covered with nail incisions on the back with a few on the front below the waist (pl. 8g), and another has horizontal lines around the waist (pl. 8b). There are only a few that end in a round flat base (pl. 8e); the others are all broken off at the waist or just below it. It is interesting to note that although the round flat base cannot be assumed for all of the examples classified here, it does exist as a possibility. All other female figures are in the seated position. The number of examples of this type is small; conclusions are therefore not possible, but it can be observed that these figures are not portrayed as pregnant.

COMPOSITE FORM (pls. 6d, 8j-l, 9, 10, and 11a-e) 305 examples

This type, due to the special way of manufacture, is represented by only one complete example on exhibit in the Tehran Museum (pl. 6d). The pieces of this example were recovered from adjacent find spots, but they fit together perfectly. The assembly of the two parts of the upper body is shown on plate 8j. It is interesting to note the plain stalk head on an otherwise anatomically explicit figure. Also of interest is the fact that there seem to have been no arms. With the fat legs providing wide hips over which the protruding stomach rests and heavy breasts above, no more is necessary to convey the concept of the pregnant female.

TORSOS

These are basically cone-shaped, sometimes modeled around a stick in order to bind this part to the legs (pl. 9f). The fragments in this group are generally medium to small with the exception of one fairly large piece (pl. 9b). Several still have strips of appliqué around the waist or depressions that show where such strips had broken off. These appliquéd strips are pressed on in the form of a g-string, which passes between the legs, curves low around the buttocks, rises over the tops of the legs, and joins below the stomach. The knot is sometimes shown at the base of the torso in back (pl. 9b). The strips are plain or, more usually, nail or short-line incised. One is covered with pin-prick punctates (pl. 10b).

The modeling of these pieces shows separate concavities on the underside where they were fitted over paired legs (cf. pl. 8j). These torsos are generally well shaped with attention to the modeling of the back and buttocks (pl. 8l). A separate stomach piece with breasts attached was sometimes made to fit onto the lap formed by the torso/leg portion (pl. 8j). The modeling of the front part of the torso was usually rather sketchy and, without the stomach piece, did not resemble a pregnant female. These torsos, however, could also have breasts attached to them; the large pendulous breasts helped to create the impression of pregnancy.

There are two excellent examples of this layering. One is the above mentioned figurine on exhibit in the Tehran Museum. The concavities under the torso show how this was modeled over the paired legs. This torso is important because it has a stalk head that ends in little double points or horns. That this realistic figure should have had an abstract head might not have been considered had not this reassembled example been found.

Plate 9a illustrates the other example in which stomach and breasts were added to the torso. Here the head was broken off, but, since there are numerous stalk fragments that end in horns, the head of this figure was probably of this abstract form as well. There are about fifty fragments of torsos and stomaches.

BREASTS

Sixty-two pieces are classified as breasts, four of which are still attached to a fragment of the torso (pl. 8k). Only four fragments are considered to be questionably classified. Ten of the breasts have nipples which are usually made by pressing a round pellet onto the tip of the pendulous form, thus flattening the pellet into a wafer. Many of these appliquéd nipples have fallen away and have left behind a shallow round depression. This is the case with the figurine in the Tehran Museum. Only one example of a nipple pellet is punctured (pl. 9c). One nipple is in the form of a thick clay pellet placed on the tip of a well-modeled breast which comes to a point. This particular piece is also covered with very fine-line striations on the upper surface (pl. 9d).

Most of the breasts in this collection are heavy and pendulous, but some are conical in shape and end in a point. Figurines other than the composite type may have had small conical applications on an otherwise flat chest (pl. 8a). This type of breast was more likely to break off and leave behind shallow round depressions which do occur on the female torso form with extended arms.

The female represented by the composite form is naked, except for the often depicted g-string or strip of appliqué low around the hips and between the legs. This is the most realistic of the female forms and the breasts reinforce this impression; they always seem to be left bare.

ARMS

There are four arm pieces that show the hand modeled with fingers. The largest example (pl. 11b) has a flattened surface where the arm was pressed onto the body and the fingers are indicated by incision. In another example more realistically modeled a separate thumb has broken off (pl. 11a).

LEGS

For the composite form, the legs are usually thick at the thighs and taper to points; four fragments show the foot by pinching the foot portion horizontally. Sometimes there is a diagonal or vertical slash incision on each side of the leg which probably depicts the bend of the knee. The larger legs usually show a hole on their inner surface where a stick or reed was used as a dowel to hold the two together. The inner surfaces are flattened where the legs were pressed together. Hence, left and right legs can be distinguished, and also distinguished from the legs of lady stalks.

Like the breasts, these paired legs are important for the realistic depiction of the naked female figure. The g-string appliqué, which is quite general, indicates a covering of the genitals while still preserving the concept of nakedness. Remains of the appliquéd strip are often found on torso fragments or on leg fragments. On plate 9b the strip is shown passing between the legs. While some of the legs are flattened on the under surface, others are arched and the buttocks are flattened or slightly concave underneath. With outstretched legs, these seated figurines were very well balanced.

For this group of paired legs there are about eighty-five right legs and eighty left legs. Forty-one of these have some traces of a g-string, while only five show additional decoration on the surface of the leg. None of these legs can be designated as a pair, with the exception of the large, fragmentary pair of legs mentioned on page 11.

HEADS

Although perforations exist on some of the torsos of the composite type which indicate the attachment of a head or some other terminus, the only head that has been found still attached to the body is that of the figurine in Tehran (pl. 6d). In addition there are three unattached heads, one questionably classified.

The first of the additional three heads is small and round in section; it most resembles a modified stalk top. This one has hair indicated by incised nail marks that come from a central part which goes from front to back (pl. 11c). The front surface or forehead seems to have flaked off. There are no features with the possible exception of tiny knob-like ears, nor is there any modeling of the face. This head can be readily associated with the composite type of female figurine.

The second head is much broader and the neck is quite thick (pl. 11d). The top is rounded and the nose is either pinched out or built up as an appliquéd strip with short brows. The eyes are formed by tiny bivalve shells that are inserted into the plastic clay and make small round convexities. The shell has broken away, but fragments remain embedded around the rims. There is no mouth nor chin, nor are there ears or hair. Due to the thickness of the neck, this head might well have belonged to the male torso type figurine.

The third head (pl. 11e), questionably so classified, has a long stalk-like neck, round in section, with a perforation in the throat that goes diagonally down toward the back. If this is indeed a head, this perforation could perhaps be due to a reinforcement which pegs the head to the body. The "face" is pinched vertically and the edge of this ridge is worn. The head angles back and the tip is broken off. There are no traces of features, either modeled or appliquéd. As a stalk-like appendage, this could have served as a head for either a composite or abstract form.

LADY STALKS—ABSTRACT FORM (pls. 11f-q and 12a-h) 102 examples

This form was first defined at Jarmo (Broman Morales 1983:381). It is a simplification of the composite type. This is achieved by taking one leg to represent a pair. The stalk body is pulled up from the back of this leg and then pressed down on top of the leg to form the stomach. The stalk body and head are tilted up and back to create a fairly slim figure which is not noticeably pregnant. Only one example of this type (pl. 11f) shows a pregnant figure with breasts. Unfortunately, the stalk body is usually broken off right at the top of the leg. The leg can be plump and triangular in side view and may suggest a bent knee (or knees). Sometimes an incised line on each side enhances this effect (pl. 11g). Other legs are long, straight, and round in section (pl. 11h, k, n). Still others are flattened so that the sides are plump (pl. 11j). The foot end is usually broken off.

Some of these legs are decorated. Instead of an appliquéd strip, one fragment has small round pellets pressed around the base of the stalk (pl. 11m). Rows of punctates and short-line or nail incisions also are used (pls. 11h, i, l-o, q and 12b, c). Here the decoration does not necessarily suggest clothing, but some sort of rule seems to pertain in that the decoration is all concentrated on the top of the leg. Since those pieces with decoration are all broken off at the end, we do not know whether the decoration extended down the leg to the foot. One vertically incised piece (pl. 11i), however, suggests that it might have.

A variation of this form has the leg coming to a blunt, boxy end like a pillow instead of coming to a point. Two feet are thus represented by the front corners and the buttocks by the two back corners (pl. 12d-f). The key figure (pl. 12d) also has a stomach fold and appliquéd breasts and therefore can be interpreted as representing a pregnant female. Other examples are much more fragmentary and do not seem to have been as explicit. One leg is deeply scored in parallel lines over the top; the last scoring goes all the way around the end of the piece and suggests a separation of the feet from the legs at the ankles (pl. 12h). There are nineteen examples of this variation.

SNAIL LADIES—ABSTRACT FORM (pls. 6e, 12i-n, 13a-o, and 14a-c) 168 examples

The leg of these figures differs from that of the lady stalk type in that it curves to one side and its under surface usually is flattened. The stalk, instead of doubling up over the back of the leg, coils around the end, clockwise or counter clockwise, before rising to form the neck and head. Some of these figurines look so much like shells, with the twisting coil suggesting that of the snail, that I named them "snail ladies."

The key example for this type (pls. 6e and 12i) is in the National Museum in Tehran. This figure does not stand well. Were it not for the plain surface underneath, it would be difficult to orient this piece. The leg or "shell" is carefully and beautifully decorated with parallel-line nail incisions which are followed by a row of tiny circular punctates that were produced by use of a hollow stem like that of a straw. The long stalk, round in section and continuing from the coil, terminates in a flattened top in a kind of turban produced by appliqué, some of which has broken off. There remains a pointed flap down one side. The leg ends with a foot that is separated from the leg by a strip of appliqué. The top surface of the foot is covered with parallel-line incisions.

Twenty-one other figurines of this type are covered with different kinds of decoration. These are in the form of parallel fine-line incision, pin pricks or circular punctates (pls. 12m, n and 13a-i). Legs with such decoration sometimes have an appliquéd pellet or strip over the ankle. Since the body form is not indicated, such as the rounding of the buttocks or the shaping of the back, the impression is of the loose Near Eastern trousers that end in a close-fitting cuff. Only the abstract forms are depicted in this fashion; therefore, their meaning may have been different from the essentially naked, more realistic composite figures. Fabric impressions have been found on some of the pieces of shaped clay (see p. 26), so it would seem logical to assume that woven textiles were worn by the people at Sarab.

A variation of this type of figurine is the bent knee type. In a few of the twenty-one examples included in the total number of snail ladies, the right leg is extended while the left leg is coiled into itself to present a knee rather than a foot (pl. 13j-m). This coil can then become more elaborate. One of these figurines has a pair of breasts appliquéd onto the body coil which tilts back (pl. 13k).

In another piece, the tip of the right leg is pinched to make a foot and the bent knee is also pinched into a foot, which make the left leg much shorter than the right. There seems to have been a change in intent on the part of the maker; the result is not very successful (pl. 13o).

The rest of the pieces of this type have the roll of clay coming up over the right leg to form a knee and continuing on to become the body stalk (pl. 13j, k, m). The stalk is broken off, but the angle of the coil shows that it must have had a stalk head. None of these figurines is decorated; they would be the simplest to make and would involve merely a roll or rope of clay. They are not as well modeled as the snail ladies; often the clay roll is cracked where it coils.

Finally, there are five examples of more complete figures. Here the legs are wrapped around to the right or to the left and provide a fairly broad and flat base on which these figures sit. Three have appliquéd breasts; one of these also has the buttocks delineated by an incision (pl. 14a-c).

There remain twenty-four fragments of coils which probably belong to this type. Only four show some form of decoration. In addition there are also twenty-four fragments of legs. Sizes range from medium/large to tiny and, in general, these figurines show a great deal of skill and care in their modeling.

STALK HEADS—ABSTRACT FORM (pl. 14d-o) 298 examples

These rod fragments have one end modified while the other end is broken off. Usually the section of the rod or stalk is round. The most common type (pl. 14d-g), with forty-nine examples, ends in double horns such as those on the illustrated composite type female figurine (pl. 8j). These little double points or horns are themselves frequently broken off. There is no other modification of the stalk—no pinching out of a face nor any appliquéd features. The stalks are usually straight, some are slightly curved or twisted; many show that they were broken off of the lady stalk form, while others could have belonged to snail ladies; although there is no whole example of this sort. The horned type of stalk head is therefore definitely associated with both the realistic composite form and the abstract form and is itself abstract.

Other rod fragments have other modifications, the most notable of which is the head of the snail lady illustrated on plates 6e and 12i. Here a flap comes down the side of the stalk head; this flap is the end of a coil of clay which has been wrapped around the flattened top of the stalk to create a kind of turban. A more clear example of this type of coil can be seen on the stalk head broken off of a snail lady. Here a pellet has been appliquéd also, presumably as a face (pl. 14j). Two other heads end in a strip of clay folded over over the top (pl. 14i, k). There may have been round pellets for the face appliquéd under these. Another small stalk has a piece of clay shaped over the top which gives the impression of a turban or bonnet (pl. 14l), while yet another has a strip wrapped around the top; the strip is decorated with vertical fine-line incisions (pl. 14m). Another example has a pinched face and a strip of clay applied across the top of the stalk and pressed down the back on both sides (pl. 14n).

A larger, thicker stalk seems to have had a rounded nose pinched out (pl. 14o). The stalk is oval in section and is flattened side to side. The head presents a triangular shape with rounded "ears" at the back. This piece suggests an animal rather than a human head.

Other forms end with the top rounded over and pressed down on the stalk (pl. 14l). It is difficult to decide how to orient these pieces; does the knob represent the face or is it the hair or turban behind the head? Since there are no features, not even punctate eyes to aid in orientation, these heads were probably not meant to be realistic. It seems obvious, therefore, that the body was what mattered. This is in contrast to the animal figurines which often have punctated eyes, mouth, and even ears; obviously the realism of the animal head was important to the maker.

Other modifications include rounded ends, sometimes with a flap turned down. The flap may be broken off and an indentation under the break shows where the missing piece was pressed against the stalk. Another group is that of the tapered tops with blunt or pointed ends. Finally, some rod sections have both ends broken off with the stalk shaped, tapered, or tapered and slightly curved. An additional few are questionably included here; they are straight-sided with the diameters and general well-made appearance fitting in well with this group. Thirteen fragments with a side or a piece of the side sheared off and with larger diameters, though with the stalks still smooth and well-made, are the last of these stalk forms that might be included in the human figurine category.

MISCELLANEOUS—ABSTRACT FORM (pls. 6f, g and 14p, q) 4 examples

Finally there are a few interesting pieces that do not fit into the types established for the human figurines nor do they form a type of their own. Fragmentary and battered, they are still worthy of mention. One small piece that is wedge-shaped is covered with nail incisions (pl. 14p). Feet are pinched out at the lower front corners while at the top back corner a tiny stalk has been broken off. The base is flat and smooth. This abstract form represents a seated figure; the upper surface of the wedge forms a lap; the upper corners over the feet are the knee. The overall decoration would seem to suggest a garment.

Another figure is a flat rounded form covered with punctates (pl. 6g). Tiny "arms" project out at the sides; a stalk head seems to have broken off at the top. The bottom and edges are rounded so that this piece would seem made to be held in the hand. This piece in Tehran was not available to me in 1978. The only information comes from the field notes and the photograph which is slightly larger than l:l. The piece measures approximately 28 mm wide by 23 mm high.

Also in Tehran on exhibit in the museum is a very simple form, a rounded triangle in shape (pl. 6f). It seems to represent a seated female whose stalk body slopes to an ample "lap" and ends with slightly divided "knees." The piece seems complete and is not part of a composite figurine. A similar form differs in that the thick stalk is bent forward to form a stomach over the thick rounded base. The upper or head end of the stalk is broken off (pl. 14q).

CONCLUSIONS

It can be seen that the manufacture of the female figurine produces forms ranging from simple to complex, in which the figure is made up of several parts that are assembled and often reinforced. The forms also vary from realistic to abstract with various forms and methods used to produce the abstract shapes. The more realistic composite forms have appliquéd strips added in the form of g-strings around the waist and between the legs. This is often shown with the strip knotted at the base of the spine. Otherwise, the figures seem to be naked. The few examples of this form that have incised lines on the leg could perhaps be considered to have been tattooed (pl. 10c, g, i). It would surely seem that there is a real difference in the treatment of decoration between the composite forms and the abstract forms.

It is to be supposed that at Sarab the human figurine did not represent a real person. Even the more realistic composite form can be considered a portrayal of a general "femaleness" since it lacks a realistic head which would personify it. It can also be conjectured that the purpose behind the modeling of each form was also different, in which case the female figurine may not have merely represented a fertility figure. They instead may be considered to be personal wish figures whose purposes may have varied and whose meaning must have varied as well.

Since so many fragments were recovered from the ashy layers of the habitation area represented by Operation I, the female figurine, even if ritually buried in the fields to give fertility to the soil, was also used for some other reason in and about the dwellings. It must be remembered that fragments of human figurines, like those of the animals, were found throughout the areas excavated, at all levels and with no particular groupings or concentrations observed.

ABSTRACT FORMS

DISCUSSION

The objects in this category are not demonstrably related to either the animal or the human figurine categories, although there may be some correlation. Stalk objects could possibly be considered close to the abstract forms of the human figurine category, while double-winged-base objects could be related to the flat-based animal figurines. This seems less likely since the base of the double-winged-base objects is often short in proportion to the height of the stalk; this is never seen in the animal figures, the base of which represents the forelegs with the back legs stretched out together, in front and in back, to make the base proportionately quite long.

The "studs" represent something new in the Sarab clay category in that there are comparable shapes in stone. These small stone and clay objects have been called "labrets" (Hole, Flannery, and Neeley 1969:235), but it is doubtful that the *clay* forms of this type at Sarab were used as such, especially since not all of them were highly polished or burnished and only some of them show wear and high polish on the base. (None of the objects classified as double-winged-base objects have worn or polished bases, although the shape is somewhat similar.) Most of the studs are quite small so that the idea of using them for buffers or smoothers does not seem plausible. The orientation for these stud-like objects is not clear. Unlike the double-winged-base objects, they do not stand on their "base."

STALK OBJECTS (pl. 15a-c, f-o) 38 examples

The predominant form here is that in the shape of a nail; the "nail head," however, is seen as a flat flared base while the shaft is a tall round-sectioned stalk that comes to a point (pl. 15a-c, f-k). Of the thirty-eight pieces in this group, five are whole (pl. 15a, b). (Two more of these pieces were unavailable to me in the Tehran Museum in 1978.) Twenty-one examples have the tip broken off. Of these, four have decoration; one has punctates around the waist (pl. 15g), two have vertical nail incisions around the edge of the base (pl. 15i), and one has multiple nail incisions over the top of the base up to the stalk (pl. 15h). There are ten base fragments; one of these is only partial and another is broken off where a row of punctations perforated the base of the stalk. There is one stalk fragment (pl. 15c). The bases are flat (in 17 examples), slightly concave (in 8 examples), or slightly convex (in 9 examples). One has a slightly grooved oval base. A line at the join on a few examples shows how the stalk was made separately and applied to the base. This method of manufacture accounts for the fact that seven of the bases have broken away from the stalk at this join. All of the pieces in this group are small, even tiny, and are carefully made.

Another group consists of ten examples only, four of which are questionably classified. These pieces, unlike the "nail," are not clearly related to the abstract human forms. With so few examples it is difficult to define these shapes. They are asymmetric and lumpy, but the bases, which are rounded or oval in plan, are not elongated enough to be double-winged-base objects (pl. 15l-o). They are rather more cone-like; the cones, however, being symmetrical, have been placed in the geometric forms category.

There are also six questionably classified stalk fragments, two with flattened, rounded tips and flattened oval sections, and four with both ends broken off. These fragments are shaped in a different way from those already discussed as stalk heads and are therefore classified here as an abstract, non-human form.

DOUBLE-WINGED-BASE OBJECTS (pl. 15p-ab) 69 examples

All of these forms, with one exception, are quite small; many are tiny. This collection may be divided into five main groups, with an additional one that contains special pieces which differ from the established types. The first group of only four is characterized by a tall pinched stalk that ends in a rounded tip (pl. 15p). Another example has the tip broken off and its base is flat and slightly convex. On three examples the base is short in proportion to the height of the stalk and the ends are rounded. The base of the example illustrated on plate 15p is long, flattened on top, and ends in sharp points.

The next type is a slight variation of the first. While the stalk is again pinched, it is more shaped and sometimes further pinched to suggest a face (pl. 15q). The tip is either rounded or comes to a point. The lower part of the stalk is often divided from the base by nail incisions (pl. 15r). Another has an appliquéd strip laid over the top at right angles to the base and pressed down the stalk to the base on either side (pl. 15s). The bases generally are flat underneath, slightly convex, and give the pieces a rocker look. Again, the base is short while the stalk is tall. Most of the twenty-four examples show the top of the base pinched up along its length to the stalk (pl. 15q, r). There are fifteen more or less whole examples and eight bases. The tip of one of these bases is folded under and pressed onto the flattened bottom. All but one of this group are tiny and very well made.

The third group differs from the second in that the stalk is more rounded in section and not pinched. There are nine pieces in this group (none illustrated), five more or less whole and four bases. The bases are flat, slightly convex, and lack nail incisions or other modifications. Basal ends are pointed and the bases are short. The top of one piece is turned over as a flap.

The fourth group, which is represented by five pieces, has the stalk pinched to the low rounded top. All examples are tiny and the bases show the rocker form. One piece (pl. 15u) has an appliquéd strip wrapped around the base of the stalk, while three others have the stalk set off from the base by nail incisions (pl. 15t). The tops of the bases are pinched up.

The fifth group, with ten examples, has a tall rounded stalk which ends in a point or a turned-over tip (pl. 15y). One piece has an appliquéd strip around the stalk at the base (pl. 15v). Another has the base pinched out at the sides below the stalk to form a long diamond in plan (pl. 15w). Again, the bases are flat and end in pointed tips or, in two cases, bluntly rounded ends. Most bases are rounded on top but two are pinched.

The final group contains six examples all of which are different. One has an appliquéd "cloak" decorated with deep pin-prick incisions pressed around the stalk (pl. 15aa). Another has a low elongated top with a long strip folded back over it (pl. 15ab). A similar shape is plain with the pinched top chipped off. A tiny rocker-based example is like the fourth type except that here the low rounded top is pinched at right angles to the base (pl. 15x). A large, rather crude fragment has a round stalk pinched front and back and appliqué on either side that forms projections or "ears" (pl. 15z). The stalk is set off from the base by nail incisions and the flat base is very curved. There is finally a very large fragment with a flat short base from which rises a thick stalk, more or less round in section. While this piece does not seem to fit into this category, in which all of the other examples are small or tiny, the base does not suggest any other classification, certainly not that of a flat-based animal figurine.

There are also eleven fragments of squashed, flattened bases or base stalk pieces with the ends broken off. While representing the form they are otherwise unclassifiable.

STUDS (pl. 16a-h) 80 examples

There are four shapes in this group. The first, a labret-shaped piece in the form that also occurs in stone, has a rounded beveled top with a double-pointed base (pl. 16a-c). The twenty-two examples are all small and eight are burnished to a hard gloss. One of these could possibly be of bone; burnt and polished, it has a mottled appearance. There are three whole examples and nineteen fragments.

The second form is similar, but the low flat top is sometimes oval rather than round (pl. 16d). The base is almost straight instead of arched as for the first form. There is a small stone stud of this shape and there are eleven examples in clay.

The third form is that of a tall pointed cone with a flat or slightly curved double-pointed base (pl. 16g). The bases are more or less oval while the stalks or cones are round in section. Seven of the eighteen pieces are smooth and highly polished. There are also six examples of this type in stone; four are triangular and two are tall cones with the tips broken off.

The last form is that of a tall thick shape with rounded top and double-pointed base; again the base is narrow and more or less oval in plan, while the body is round in section (pl. 16e, f). There are two pieces of this form in stone, one almost whole and the other fragmentary. A highly polished or burnished surface occurs on five of the fourteen examples. There is a small collection of tips and points which may belong to this group of studs; there are six tips and nine points. All are black and highly polished or burnished.

There may be a few more of these studs, in stone and in clay, in the Tehran Museum; only one example in clay of the first form was seen in the museum laboratory collection in 1978.

CONCLUSIONS

This remains an enigmatic category; labret-shaped clay objects do not make much sense when the form is represented by examples made of stone. It is possible that the shape itself has a meaning or significance beyond that of personal adornment, in which case the clay "labrets" need not have been actually worn. The double-winged-base objects show no sign of polishing and are also very small so that their use as buffers or smoothers is not likely. The use of any of these forms as counters or gaming pieces is improbable since neither the double-winged-base objects nor the studs stand well. Given the small size of the sample, not much can be deduced from it. There may be relationships either with the abstract human forms or with the purely geometric forms, of course.

GEOMETRIC FORMS (pls. 15d, e; 16i-t; and 17a-k)

DISCUSSION

In this category are balls, flattened discs, cones, tetrahedrons, blocks and oblongs, rod fragments, and rolled pieces. Balls occur in almost every collection of shaped clay material. These can be easily assessed as counters or marbles and seem to have little to do with the wish-magic implications of the figurine material so far discussed. Some of the balls are incised in various ways, perhaps to show multiple rather than unit value. That counters were used to aid in control of flocks taken daily to pasture is quite probable. Small pebbles could have served the same purpose, but plastic clay could be more readily modeled to give the desired size and number. Shepherds could also have used balls for games of marbles while tending the flocks. The present-day workers at Jarmo, when asked what they thought the balls were, used a finger-flicking technique more suited to the small size than the knuckle-shooting one that I was familiar with. Diameters for these balls range from 7-15 mm. Larger balls are either faceted (not true spheres) or are only fragments. The use of clay balls as sling missiles is another obvious explanation and could account for the hard smooth-surfaced faceted balls of various sizes. One assumes that a bag or pouch was used as a container. Stone balls of various sizes also were found.

The flattened discs also could have served as counters where a ball would not have been convenient. Gaming pieces could be another use conjectured for these. They could also have been casually formed, rather like doodles in clay, as the rolled pieces must surely have been. Some of the discs show impressions on the flattened side and have many straw inclusions.

The cones and related tetrahedrons are another matter; only because their relationship to the abstract human figurines cannot yet be demonstrated have they been placed in this category. Other pieces may someday be recovered that will definitely show that that is where they belong. One step in that direction, perhaps, is the decorated wedge-shaped figurine (pl. 14p and see p. 18). However, none of the tetrahedrons at Sarab has any decoration. Some of the cones, classified as "nails," do show different forms of decoration around the base (pl. 15g-i).

The cones and tetrahedrons are considered with the geometric forms. Both types could have been used as counters or gaming pieces since they stand very well.

The blocks and oblongs present the same problem in interpretation. For the most part they are nicely modeled and some of them are decorated. At the moment the gaming piece or counter is all that suggests itself.

BALLS (pl. 17a-c) 79 examples

These come in all sizes and can be smooth and nicely rounded or lumpy and uneven. Some are faceted and others show signs of having been rolled between the palms. Some examples were carefully prepared and then incised; others were carelessly formed and show pebble inclusions. The smaller balls (diameters of 8.5-15 mm) were probably used as counters or marbles—or both. The very few incised balls might have represented a multiple value in their use as counters. Sling missiles, especially for the hunting of birds as observed in the area today, is another suggested use. D. Jánussy in Bökönyi (1977:119-30) reports the bones of many species of birds in the faunal remains found at Sarab.

It is difficult to give figures for the clay balls as so many classified here are only fragments and may represent parts of some other form. They can be roughly divided by size: fifty-eight in the 7-15 mm range, fourteen in the 16-24 mm range, and five in the 26-40 mm range. There are also two very large balls with a diameter of 60 mm.

FLATTENED DISCS (pl. 17d-g) 123 examples

These come in various forms: plano-convex, bi-convex, bi-plano, bi-concave, and concavo-convex. Sizes range from tiny lentoid shapes to very large ones. These discs may represent counters or mere doodles. Some, especially the smaller examples, are nicely shaped and smoothed, whereas others are indifferently fashioned and show fibrous inclusions on their rough and cracked exteriors. Only a few have any modification of the surface. One very smooth bi-plano fragment has a row of short gash punctates over the upper surface (pl. 17e). About fifty pieces have been placed in this division.

CONES (pls. 15d, e and 16i-o) 76 examples

This form can be divided into seven groups. The first group is the ogival cone with straight, proportionately low sloping sides that end in a pointed top (pl. 16i, j). All are nicely made and smooth. The tips of all but three are broken off. The nine examples are all small (basal diameter ca. 13 mm) and have flat bases. One exception has a slightly concave base and a row of punctates all around parallel to the base.

The next group is similar—squat but with thick basal edges—and the examples are not well made. There are only seven of these and all but one of them are larger than those of the first group. Three of the bases are flat and four are concave.

The third set consists of twenty pieces; half of them come to a rounded tip while the tips of the others are broken off. The cone tapers almost without any flaring of the base, as is true also of the first two groups. The bases are flat or slightly concave (five examples). These cones are not as carefully made as the first two groups.

The fourth group is characterized by a tall stalk that rises from a flared base (pl. 15d, e). The cone ends in a rounded or pointed tip. The stalk is more or less round in section; few of this type show careful modeling. There are twenty examples, eleven of which are whole and the remainder have part of the stalk broken off. One of the latter has parallel nail incisions slanted around the base.

The fifth group of only four examples is a squat form with low rounded top and round flat base. This rather resembles a gumdrop; only one is polished or burnished (pl. 16k). The sides slope with little or no shaping, unlike the next set in which the form is definitely waisted or restricted just above the base.

The sixth group is a waisted form, short and plump, with a rounded top. The five examples of this low form, all fragmentary, are small (pl. 16l, o), except for a large fragment whose greatest basal diameter is 26 mm. The surface of the stalk of this piece seems to have been raked in a series of shallow parallel lines. The surface is otherwise quite smooth and polished as is the slightly convex base. The waisting is very pronounced, with the indentation quite low on the stalk which rounds up or swells immediately above this waist. The bases of all examples are flat and very smooth.

The last group of cones is represented by eleven examples. These are also waisted but are taller pieces (pl. 16m, n), also only fragments. All have highly polished or burnished surfaces. The waisting here is generally faceted and the stalk rises without the bulging of the previous form. One piece (pl. 16m) shows a vertical scraping down to the line that marks the waist. A line and faceting mark the other illustrated piece.

TETRAHEDRONS (pl. 16p-s) 40 examples

The forty examples are all more or less whole except for four fragments. Two examples show one edge turned over and pressed down in the making (pl. 16q), while two others of the same size are asymmetrical and have one tip broken off. There are two smaller pieces, only one of which, a corner and possibly broken off of something else, is questionably classified. The size range is great, from 45 mm high to only 9 mm. There are five examples whose basal side length is from 24-28 mm. The height of these is about 25 mm. There follow seven pieces with basal side length ranging from 19-23 mm whose height is from 18-24 mm. Two pieces 15-16 mm height and 17-18 mm basal side length (e.g., pl. 16p) separate the larger tetrahedrons from the smaller ones. These are then roughly divided into two groups: basal size from 13-14 and from 9-12 mm. Overall height of these smaller tetrahedrons is from 9-13 mm. There are twelve pieces in the first group and five in the last one. The asymmetrical examples are about 16 mm wide by 16 mm high. All examples but three are more or less equal sided. These exceptions are the largest one (basal length 34-36 mm and estimated height 45 mm), another tall and slim one, which is very well made with flat base and very slightly concave sides (pl. 16s), and a tall, spire-like example (pl. 16r) whose triangular shaped stalk is restricted above the base though with no interruption in the angles of the sides.

All tetrahedrons have flat or very slightly concave bases in contrast to the sides which are generally concave to some degree. This is due to the shaping by fingers which pressed into the sides as the piece was held on a flat surface.

BLOCKS, OBLONGS, AND MISCELLANEOUS RELATED FORMS (pls. 16t and 17h-k) 70 exx.

There are sixteen examples of rectangular shaped blocks, five of which have some sort of incised decoration (pl. 17h-k). There are also ten oblongs and seventeen fragments of oblongs with one end broken off. These are more or less oval in section. There are also fragments of oblongs that are flattened side to side, plano-convex, and bi-plano.

In the group of miscellaneous shaped forms, there are two tapered cylinders, both of which are complete pieces. One is tall, straight, and ends in a rounded point; it looks like a small pestle (pl. 16t); the other is curved and twisted. Both have flat round bases. Two small black burnished fragments may also be considered here. One is a split piece that is shaped and slightly twisted. The other is smaller and seems to have been spool-shaped. This could perhaps have been a stud fragment. Another group of tapered cylinders with one end flattened has eighteen examples.

Another group of rod sections generally have larger cross-sections than those of the stalk type. These are round in section or have one flattened side or are faceted. There are twenty-three of these. Finally there is a small collection of forty rolled pieces. These are generally small with ends that come to pointed tips, as clay must when rolled back and forth between the palms. The surface of all these pieces is not smoothed as it is for the shaped and modeled objects but is rough because of inclusions or air holes.

CONCLUSIONS

Little can be added to the discussion of the balls and flattened discs which are considered as part of the counter/gaming piece category. The same can be said for the blocks, while the oblongs and miscellaneous forms are very hard to interpret. The cones, however, are highly specialized and seem to have a significance other than that of mere counters or gaming pieces. The small size (which requires careful modeling and finishing, even burnishing of some of the forms) serves to set these pieces apart from the other geometric forms. I should be inclined to consider the cones as probably related to the abstract human figurine forms.

As for the tetrahedrons, those pieces that were deformed in the making (pl. 16q) lead to speculation as to the use or purpose of this form. If they were to be used as counters or gaming pieces, would they not have been re-formed while the clay was still plastic? Actually, in view of the proliferation of female figures elaborated in abstract forms, especially the wedge-shaped piece, (see p. 18 and pl. 14p) there is no reason why these very nicely shaped polyhedrons could not also be placed in that category. The tetrahedrons are best left in this group, however, until further examination of this form in other collections leads to a more definite conclusion.

PERFORATED FORMS

BEADS AND PENDANT (pl. 17l-n) 5 examples

As for beads, there are only four of clay in this division. Two of the beads are small and long, flattened barrel shaped (pl. 17l, m; only half of 17m remains). The third, a pendant-like bead, is also a long barrel shape, but the perforation here runs through the top part only (pl. 17n). All three of these objects are hard, smooth surfaced, and well made. A more or less round, flattened lump of clay has been pierced asymmetrically toward one edge. This piece is battered and faceted; it was not carefully made. The last example, that of a pendant, is roughly rectangular, flattened in section, and perforated at each end by passing a straw at an angle through the wet clay. Both perforations slant the same way. The surface of this pendant is irregular with deep grass impressions on one surface.

There were several beads of stone so that it seems strange to find beads made of clay at all when stone beads were being made and would have been much more desirable.

MISCELLANEOUS OBJECTS (pl. 17o-u)

Although textile impressions have been found on some of the clay fragments, only four perforated objects can be classified as spindle whorls. The diameters of the perforations are 4-5 mm and, although all three are fragments, they were probably symmetrical. The perforations were built up or "collared" on one or both sides. Diameters range from 32-50 mm.

Twenty others, half of them more or less whole, cannot have been whorls because of the small size of the perforation, occasionally off center, and the asymmetrical shape of the object. The diameters of these range from 24-30 mm with most of them in the 25-26 mm range (pl. 17p-r). One of the fragments, plano-convex in section, is covered with vertical rows of finger-nail incisions (pl. 17u). Otherwise these forms are plain and finger-faceted in shaping. They have been pushed out of symmetry while still plastic or the perforation was not centered. Most of these perforations are collared on both sides. Since spindle whorls were probably made of wood or shaped from pot sherds, it is not surprising that so few are represented in modeled clay.

Other perforated objects of note are illustrated (pl. 17o, s, t). They were only partially perforated; the hole does not completely pierce the object. In the case of the spool-like piece illustrated on plate 17o, the hole may have been accidental, a blow-out rather than planned; it is centered, however.

No suggestion as to use or meaning can be given; the pieces classified here are fairly carefully modeled. A possible wish-magic use could be conjectured for the small whorl-like objects since they were misshapen in their plastic state. If so, they are abstract forms.

MISCELLANEOUS FORMS

TEXTILE, MAT, AND BASKET IMPRESSIONS (pl. 18) 8 examples

There are two fragments of clay that show impressions of what may have been sections of baskets (pl. 18 h, j). One looks like the center coil of the base while another in stronger relief may be the side. An irregular surface impression may represent a split-reed basket or mat (pl. 18g). Two small fragments of clay show very clear impressions of twill matting (pl. 18d, e).

A simple gauze weave (one warp thread, one woof thread) can be seen on two small clay fragments (pl. 18a, b). The example of textile (pl. 18c) shows a double thread in one direction and a single thread in the other. There are not enough examples of fabric impression to conclude anything about the use of cloth.

The very complicated patterns created by punctates and incisions as seen on the snail ladies (see p. 16) obviously indicate some sort of body decoration even if that were only body paint or tattooing.

VARIED PIECES

Spoon fragments may be represented by four small pieces; one looks like a handle at the point where it broadens into the bowl, while the other three are concavo-convex pieces with a thin edge.

Five flat based pieces may be miniature vessel fragments. The side rises directly from the base on one example, while the others show a waist that is pinched out just above the base. There are two rim sherds tapered to a rounded lip and four small concavo-convex body sherds.

SHAPED CLAY PIECES

There are many fragments which are concavo-convex, as though formed around a thick stick; they are all broken lengthwise. About 540 fragments are placed in this group.

There is finally a large collection (estimated at about 15 cubic decimeters) of pieces of shaped clay. These show some modeling but are not classifiable; most are fragmentary. These pieces may be the hardened remains of the plastic raw material used in the manufacture of the figurines.

All of the clay objects classified and discussed in this report are made of fine-grained clay, possibly that which silts out on the banks of rivers and wadis. Not much clay was needed at any one time for the production of figurines, unlike the clay used for pottery which would also have been processed in a different way. Some sort of temper was needed for the larger pottery pieces, otherwise they would crack or break in firing.

Since the figurines had no utility, their treatment after manufacture seems to have been casual, however well or poorly realized those objects were. It was the act of modeling the plastic clay that was important, as the figurines themselves have now demonstrated.

COMPARATIVE ANALYSIS OF SARAB AND JARMO FIGURINES

In terms of dating, Sarab is considered to be about five hundred years later than Jarmo. Their physical settings (Jarmo-Chemchemal Valley: Sarab-Kermanshah Valley) are very similar; they occupy a similar ecological niche although Sarab is well up in the Zagros Range and Jarmo only on the Zagros Piedmont. At both sites animal husbandry was practiced while hunting of wild animals was still carried out. In fact, Bökönyi gives hunting equal importance with the tending of domestic flocks in his report on the faunal evidence at Sarab. Wild sheep and goats and wild pigs were present in both valleys. Gazelle bones were found in numbers at Sarab. Figurines show that dogs were present at both sites; at Sarab, Bökönyi reports the bones of dogs and wild wolf/dogs. (For a general discussion of the domesticated dog, see Lawrence and Reed 1983.)

Great concentrations of the shells of a local land snail (*Helix salomonica*) occur in both places and surely indicate the use of this mollusk for food. Grains in wild form still exist in the Chemchemal valley, and wild barley but not wheat is found in the Kermanshah valley. Therefore a hunting/gathering economy clearly underlies the early settlements and continues along with the domestication of animals and the cultivation of grains. Hunting provides more than meat, of course; there are hides, skins, and bones and horn for tools and weapons. Textile impressions of fine linen weaves are found at both sites and show that vegetable fibers were spun into thread and woven into cloth.

The occupation patterns of Jarmo and Sarab, however, greatly differ. Although later in time, Sarab seems to have consisted of a series of small oval semi-pit structures roofed with perishable materials; all that remains is an ashy layering in levels going down to 1.5 -2 m.

Jarmo, though earlier, is clearly in the primary village stage with mud-walled architecture; this is in the form of well-built rectilinear walled houses of several rooms in some of which occurred baked-in-place clay basins and ovens. There is also the evidence at both sites of the cereal grains themselves (wheat and barley) and many stone mortars and pestles.

The state of preservation of the lightly baked clay figurine material at Sarab is comparable only to that of the ash area at Jarmo, where a great quantity of figurine fragments was recovered. (The ashy levels of habitation at Sarab contained almost the whole sample of clay figurine material from that site.) Otherwise the soil at Jarmo is compacted and the upper half meter is leached by water percolation which has seriously affected the clay material, pottery as well as figurines.

The figurine collections themselves are highly comparable (for those of Jarmo, see Broman Morales 1983). Both collections show about the same categories; the later material from Sarab is more elaborated and contains a few new forms. The animal figurines show the same emphasis on wild forms, all of which are not identifiable. The modeling of the animals changes; the flat base is used for many of the various forms at Sarab. None of the Jarmo figures has a flat base. The human figurines, with realistic and abstract forms appearing at both sites, show added forms at Sarab with the snail lady and related forms the most important. The appliquéd g-string, itself sometimes adorned by fine-line incising or punctates, on the composite female forms and also the elaborate decoration on the snail ladies contrast with the lack of such adornment on the Jarmo female figures.

There are many more separate heads in the Jarmo collection; features, for the Jarmo people, seem to have been important. This factor has apparently disappeared almost completely by Sarab times. Another difference is in the depiction of the male figure. At Jarmo, male figurines are better defined and there are several phallic objects in both clay and stone. At Sarab, the male figures are small in size as well as few in number.

The double-winged-base object and the stalk object categories, so prominent in the Jarmo collection, are quite residual by Sarab times. Either some other form took their place or the meaning and purpose of these objects were no longer pertinent. New forms such as studs and decorated bricks or blocks have yet to be interpreted.

In summary, while the Sarab material would seem to be about 500 years later than that of Jarmo, there is a clear continuum in the manufacture and some of the forms of the clay figurines. Each site seems to have been occupied over a period of several hundred years. Therefore this continuum may represent 600-700 years. It would certainly seem that the continued importance of hunting even in Sarab times preserved the tradition of the modeling of wish figures by individuals as the need arose. That not all of the figures so modeled had to do with hunting is quite apparent, but the need for magic in hunting success could be seen as carrying through into the manufacture of non-animal objects. Each person seems to have created his or her own wish figures and formed a tangible object out of intangible thoughts or wishes.

CONCLUSIONS

Theoretical Concepts Of Clay Figurine Manufacture

From the earliest manifestations of primitive art, it can be seen that early people were concerned with controlling their environment. They invented their own magic—tokens, signs, and symbols—which gave them, to their mind at least, control over the terrifying manifestations of nature and the often fearsome beasts which they had to hunt and kill in order to survive. Hunting and gathering groups must of necessity be limited in numbers. Undoubtedly the birth rate was low and life expectancy short. By the time that they had advanced enough to live in permanent settlements, because of the more or less stable food supply available through agriculture and animal domestication, they could be more comfortable about their place in the natural scheme of things. They had begun to be able to control their environment.

Could the time now have come when they could think in terms of their own wants and needs? It is probably at this period that the first small clay objects were made with the idea that the magic or the wish was incorporated in the clay as the piece was formed. Each person did her/his own wish-magic with the clay. In giving plastic expression to their thoughts, they were giving tangible form to their intangible ideas in a way as important as writing. The existence of fragments of these clay objects today gives a tantalizing and fascinating view of the world view and the self-view of these early settlers some 8000 years ago.

While disappointingly fragmentary for the most part, occasional key pieces show what the whole object must have looked like. After dealing with thousands of these fragments, it is possible to perceive how the modelers abstracted the animal and human figures, especially the latter. It is not possible, however, to tell whether these abstract forms expressed the same or different ideas as those of the more realistic forms. (Both the realistic and abstract figures are found in the same levels and do not represent a development of the one from the other through time.) What seems to be indicated is an articulateness in abstract thought and concepts that could presuppose an advanced verbal capacity as well.

At the early village level the number of people living together could increase. Probably the birth rate rose as a more stable food supply gave nourishment and strength to the villagers. Women, as bearers of the children who were necessary for the continued success of the village, could have been considered more important and were to be protected from harm. They undoubtedly made their own wish figures to ensure their personal well-being, successful pregnancies, and live births. If they also herded the animals and prepared the food, in addition to having sown and harvested the crops, they obviously played a very prominent part in the village life and economy. The men were the builders, tool makers, and hunters; since a large part of their subsistence would still have come from hunting. As game retreated from areas near human settlements, this would take them farther away from the villages. It can be suggested that the men, therefore, would model the figures of the wild animals that they desired to kill or capture while the women would perhaps make the figures of the herded domestic animals that were in their care.

It is not possible to ascertain whether there were fertility figurines for the fields. If there indeed were, it can be assumed that they were buried in the fields themselves and not left around the hearths in the dwellings of the village. Therefore, no figurine has yet been identified with the prosperity of the crops.

Since the clay figurines of Jarmo and Sarab were found scattered throughout the living areas at random—no concentrations or special buildings are associated with them—and in obvious dump areas, it seems certain that these objects were not intended for permanency or re-use, seasonally or occasionally. The pregnant female figurines found in habitation areas must have had to do with human fertility only.

The fact that both the Jarmo and Sarab villagers produced beautifully worked stone objects such as bowls, bracelets, beads, and balls of various sizes indicates the ability to produce stone figurines. None such have been found, however, which argues for a deliberate impermanency of the objects modeled in clay. Each of these small objects must have been personal and individually created with the wish-magic worked in as the plastic clay took shape.

Religion at this early village stage was probably not organized. The recognition of a power greater than that of man is surely manifested by the production of the clay figurines; these were the concrete expression of thought that were controlled by personal needs and circumstances and directed to a super-human power.

It would seem that organized religion developed through a combination of factors. Those who were most successful in life, those whose wish figures seemed to work—the hunter who came back with the game for which he had wished, the woman with many healthy children and a prosperous flock—could have been asked by others, not as fortunate, to create wish figures for them. In this way, the more successful could have become specialists and, due to their superior knowledge which gave them their success in the first place, would then be in a position to act as seers and sorceresses as the villages grew.

Another very important factor was the need for social control. As more people, not related to each other through family ties, gathered in the ever-growing communities, specialization in occupation took place; specialists were paid for their services in goods or other services. Social restraints became necessary as surplus goods accumulated and some people had more than others. As more and more people crowded together in urban centers and more and more activities took place there, social control became increasingly necessary and important.

Leisure time also developed and allowed those in more favorable circumstances to reflect and to consider philosophical ideas, to speculate on the creation of earth and of mankind. Life had become much more complex than it was in early village times. One's success could no longer be considered a personal matter to be dealt with by each individual on a one-to-one basis with a superior power.

As the city centers were organized, the lives of the inhabitants too were organized in various ways and for various reasons. One of these ways was religion. This is far beyond the days of the early villagers who were still able to express their individual thoughts in a tangible form and left that tantalizing evidence in their clay figurines. Could this be considered the earliest form of human expression, as it appears with an archaeological catalog of other aspects of their daily lives? Most cave art and many petroglyphs obviously pre-date clay figurines, but their expression is isolated and dating is difficult. The clay figurines, however, were found with a welter of other information about the makers and their way of life, thus more scope in the interpretation of their expression is given.

CATALOG 1

Illustrated Figurines and Clay Objects from Sarab

Plate	*Classification*	*Findspot*
1a	Animal Figurine: Curly-Tailed Dog	SI, sf-1
1b	Animal Figurine: Curly-Tailed Dog	SIw, sf-1
1c	Animal Figurine: Curly-Tailed Dog	SI, sf-1
1d	Animal Figurine: Curly-Tailed Dog	SIc, 2ab
1e	Animal Figurine: Curly-Tailed Dog	SI, sf-1
1f	Animal Figurine: Curly-Tailed Dog	SI, sf-1
1g	Animal Figurine: Curly-Tailed Dog	SI, 2
1h	Animal Figurine: Curly-Tailed Dog	SI(?)
1i	Animal Figurine: Curly-Tailed Dog	SI, pit
1j	Animal Figurine: Curly-Tailed Dog	SIw, sf-1
1k	Animal Figurine: Curly-Tailed Dog	SI, sf-1
1l	Animal Figurine: Curly-Tailed Dog	SI, 2
1m	Animal Figurine: Curly-Tailed Dog	SI, 1
2a	Animal Figurine: Wild Pig	SI, 1
2b	Animal Figurine: Wild Pig	SIc, 2a
2c	Animal Figurine: Wild Pig	SI, 1
2d	Animal Figurine: Wild Pig	SI, sf-1
2e	Animal Figurine: Wild Pig	SIc, 2a
2f	Animal Figurine: Wild Pig	SIc, 2
2g	Animal Figurine: Wild Pig	SI, 2
2h	Animal Figurine: Wild Pig	SIc, 2a
3a	Animal Figurine: Horned	SI, 2
3b	Animal Figurine: Horned	SI, 2
3c	Animal Figurine: Horned	SI, 2
3d	Animal Figurine: Horned	SI, sf-l
3e	Animal Figurine: Horned	SIw, 1
3f	Animal Figurine: Horned	SV, 4
3g	Animal Figurine: Horned	SI, sf-1
3h	Animal Figurine: Horned	SI, sf-1
3i	Animal Figurine: Horned	SIc, 2c

Catalog 1. Illustrated Figurines and Clay Objects from Sarab—cont.

Plate	*Classification*	*Findspot*
3j	Animal Figurine: Horned	SI, 2j
3k	Animal Figurine: Horned	SI, sf-1
3l	Animal Figurine: Horned	SI, sf-1
3m	Animal Figurine: Horned	SI, 2
4a	Animal Figurine: With Tail Up	SI, 1
4b	Animal Figurine: With Tail Up	SI, 1+
4c	Animal Figurine: With Tail Up	SIc, 2b
4d	Animal Figurine: With Tail Out	SIw, sf-1
4e	Animal Figurine: With Tail Out	SIw, sf-1
4f	Animal Figurine: With Tail Out	SI, sf-1
4g	Animal Figurine: With Tail Out	SI, 3
4h	Animal Figurine: With Tail Out	SI, sf-1
4i	Animal Figurine: With Tail Out	SV, 5
4j	Animal Figurine: With Tail Out	SIc, 4
4k	Animal Figurine: With Tail Out	SI, 2
4l	Animal Figurine: With Tail Down	SI, sf-1
4m	Animal Figurine: With Tail Down	SI, sf-1
4n	Animal Figurine: With Tail Down	SI, 1a
4o	Animal Figurine: With Tail Down	SI, sf-1
5a	Animal Figurine: Non-Classifiable Fragment	SI, sf-1
5b	Animal Figurine: Non-Classifiable Fragment	SI, sf-1
5c	Animal Figurine: Non-Classifiable Fragment	SI, sf-1
5d	Animal Figurine: Non-Classifiable Fragment	SI, sf-1
5e	Animal Figurine: Non-Classifiable Fragment	SIc, 3
5f	Animal Figurine: Non-Classifiable Fragment	SIc, 2a
5g	Animal Figurine: Non-Classifiable Fragment	SIc, 2a
5h	Animal Figurine: Non-Classifiable Fragment	SIc, 2a
5i	Animal Figurine: Non-Classifiable Fragment	SIw, sf-1
5j	Animal Figurine: Non-Classifiable Fragment	SI, pit
5k	Animal Figurine: Non-Classifiable Fragment	SI, sf-1
5l	Animal Figurine: Non-Classifiable Fragment	SI, 1+
5m	Animal Figurine: Non-Classifiable Fragment	SI, sf-1
5n	Animal Figurine: Non-Classifiable Fragment	SI, sf-1
5o	Animal Figurine: Non-Classifiable Fragment	SI, sf-1
5p	Animal Figurine: Non-Classifiable Fragment	SI, sf-1
5q	Animal Figurine: Non-Classifiable Fragment	SI, sf-1
6a	Animal Figurine: Wild Pig	SI, 1
6b	Animal Figurine: Wild Pig	SI, 2
6c	Animal Figurine: Non-Classifiable Fragment	SIc, 2
6d	Human Figurine: Composite Form	SI, 2

Catalog 1. Illustrated Figurines and Clay Objects from Sarab—cont.

Plate	*Classification*	*Findspot*
6e	Abstract Form: "Snail Lady" Figurine	SI, 2
6f	Miscellaneous Type of Human Figurine	SI, sf-1
6g	Miscellaneous Type of Human Figurine	SI, 3
7a	Human Figurine: Simple Extended Form	SI, 1
7b	Human Figurine: Simple Extended Form	SI, sf-1
7c	Human Figurine: Simple Seated Form	SIw, sf-1
7d	Human Figurine: Simple Seated Form	SI, 1a
7e	Human Figurine: Simple Seated Form	SI, sf-1
7f	Human Figurine: Simple Seated Form	SI, sf-1
7g	Human Figurine: Simple Seated Form	SI, 2b
7h	Human Figurine: Simple Seated Form	SIc, 2b
7i	Human Figurine: Male Torso With Extended Arms	SI, 1
7j	Human Figurine: Male Torso With Extended Arms	SI, sf-1
7k	Human Figurine: Male Torso With Extended Arms	SI, sf-1
7l	Human Figurine: Male Torso With Extended Arms	SI, sf-1
7m	Human Figurine: Male Torso With Extended Arms	SIc, 2a
7n	Human Figurine: Male Torso With Extended Arms	SIc, 2
7o	Human Figurine: Male Torso With Extended Arms	SI, sf-1
8a	Human Figurine: Female Torso With Extended Arms	SI, sf-1
8b	Human Figurine: Female Torso With Extended Arms	SI, sf-1
8c	Human Figurine: Female Torso With Extended Arms	SIc, 2a
8d	Human Figurine: Female Torso With Extended Arms	SIc, 2a
8e	Human Figurine: Female Torso With Extended Arms	SIc, 2b
8f	Human Figurine: Female Torso With Extended Arms	SI, 2b
8g	Human Figurine: Female Torso With Extended Arms	SI, 2
8h	Human Figurine: Female Torso With Extended Arms	SI, 2a
8i	Human Figurine: Female Torso With Extended Arms	SI, sf-1
8j	Human Figurine: Composite Form, Female Torso Fragment	SI, 2
8k	Human Figurine: Composite Form, Female Breast Fragment	SI, sf-1
8l	Human Figurine: Composite Form, Female Torso Fragment	SI, sf-1
9a	Human Figurine: Composite Form, Female Torso Fragment	SI, 3
9b	Human Figurine: Composite Form, Female Torso Fragment	SI, sf-1
9c	Human Figurine: Composite Form, Female Breast Fragment	SIc, 2a
9d	Human Figurine: Composite Form, Female Breast Fragment	SI, sf-1
9e	Human Figurine: Composite Form, Female Breast Fragment	SI, 1
9f	Human Figurine: Composite Form, Female Torso Fragment	SIc, 2a
9g	Human Figurine: Composite Form, Female Torso Fragment	SIc, 2a
9h	Human Figurine: Composite Form, Female Breast Fragment	SI, sf-l
10a	Human Figurine: Composite Form, Female Leg Fragment	SI, 2
10b	Human Figurine: Composite Form, Female Leg Fragment	SIw, sf-1

Catalog 1. Illustrated Figurines and Clay Objects from Sarab—cont.

Plate	*Classification*	*Findspot*
10c	Human Figurine: Composite Form, Female Leg Fragment	SI, 2b
10d	Human Figurine: Composite Form, Female Leg Fragment	SI, sf-1
10e	Human Figurine: Composite Form, Female Leg Fragment	SI, 1
10f	Human Figurine: Composite Form, Female Leg Fragment	SI, sf-1
10g	Human Figurine: Composite Form, Female Leg Fragment	SI, sf-1
10h	Human Figurine: Composite Form, Female Leg Fragment	SI, sf-1
10i	Human Figurine: Composite Form, Female Leg Fragment	SI, sf-1
10j	Human Figurine: Composite Form, Female Leg Fragment	SI, 2
11a	Human Figurine: Composite Form, Arm Fragment	SI, 1a
11b	Human Figurine: Composite Form, Arm Fragment	SI, 1
11c	Human Figurine: Composite Form, Head Fragment	SI, sf-1
11d	Human Figurine: Composite Form, Head Fragment	SIc, 2b
11e	Human Figurine: Composite Form, Head Fragment	SI, 2b
11f	Human Figurine: Abstract Form, "Lady Stalk" Fragment	SIc, 2a
11g	Human Figurine: Abstract Form, "Lady Stalk" Fragment	SI, sf-1
11h	Human Figurine: Abstract Form, "Lady Stalk" Fragment	SI, 1a
11i	Human Figurine: Abstract Form, "Lady Stalk" Fragment	SI, sf-1
11j	Human Figurine: Abstract Form, "Lady Stalk" Fragment	SI, sf-1
11k	Human Figurine: Abstract Form, "Lady Stalk" Fragment	SI, 3
11l	Human Figurine: Abstract Form, "Lady Stalk" Fragment	SI, 3
11m	Human Figurine: Abstract Form, "Lady Stalk" Fragment	SI, sf-1
11n	Human Figurine: Abstract Form, "Lady Stalk" Fragment	SI, 1
11o	Human Figurine: Abstract Form, "Lady Stalk" Fragment	SI, 2
11p	Human Figurine: Abstract Form, "Lady Stalk" Fragment	SI, 3
11q	Human Figurine: Abstract Form, "Lady Stalk" Fragment	SI, 3
12a	Human Figurine: Abstract Form, "Lady Stalk" Fragment	SI, sf-1
12b	Human Figurine: Abstract Form, "Lady Stalk" Fragment	SI, sf-1
12c	Human Figurine: Abstract Form, "Lady Stalk" Fragment	SI, pit
12d	Human Figurine: Abstract Form, "Lady Stalk" Fragment	SIc, 2a
12e	Human Figurine: Abstract Form, "Lady Stalk" Fragment	SI, 2
12f	Human Figurine: Abstract Form, "Lady Stalk" Fragment	SI, 3
12g	Human Figurine: Abstract Form, "Lady Stalk" Fragment	SIc, 2a
12h	Human Figurine: Abstract Form, "Lady Stalk" Fragment	SI, 2
12i	Human Figurine: Abstract Form, "Snail Lady"	SI, 2
12j	Human Figurine: Abstract Form, "Snail Lady" Fragment	SI, 3
12k	Human Figurine: Abstract Form, "Snail Lady" Fragment	SI, 3
12l	Human Figurine: Abstract Form, "Snail Lady" Fragment	SV, 5
12m	Human Figurine: Abstract Form, "Snail Lady" Fragment	SI, 4
12n	Human Figurine: Abstract Form, "Snail Lady" Fragment	SI, test trench
13a	Human Figurine: Abstract Form, "Snail Lady" Fragment	SIw, 1

Catalog 1. Illustrated Figurines and Clay Objects from Sarab—cont.

Plate	*Classification*	*Findspot*
13b	Human Figurine: Abstract Form, "Snail Lady" Fragment	SI, sf-1
13c	Human Figurine: Abstract Form, "Snail Lady" Fragment	SI, sf-1
13d	Human Figurine: Abstract Form, "Snail Lady" Fragment	SIc, 2a
13e	Human Figurine: Abstract Form, "Snail Lady" Fragment	SIc, 4
13f	Human Figurine: Abstract Form, "Snail Lady" Fragment	SI, sf-1
13g	Human Figurine: Abstract Form, "Snail Lady" Fragment	SIc, 3
13h	Human Figurine: Abstract Form, "Snail Lady" Fragment	SI, 4
13i	Human Figurine: Abstract Form, "Snail Lady" Fragment	SI, 2
13j	Human Figurine: Abstract Form, "Snail Lady" Fragment	SIw, sf-1
13k	Human Figurine: Abstract Form, "Snail Lady" Fragment	SIc, 2a
13l	Human Figurine: Abstract Form, "Snail Lady" Fragment	SIc, 2a
13m	Human Figurine: Abstract Form, "Snail Lady" Fragment	SI. sf-1
13n	Human Figurine: Abstract Form, "Snail Lady" Fragment	SI, sf-1
13o	Human Figurine: Abstract Form, "Snail Lady" Fragment	SI, 2
14a	Human Figurine: Abstract Form, "Snail Lady" Fragment	SIc, 2a
14b	Human Figurine: Abstract Form, "Snail Lady" Fragment	SI, 1
14c	Human Figurine: Abstract Form, "Snail Lady" Fragment	SIc. 2b
14d	Human Figurine: Abstract Form, "Stalk" Head Fragment	SI, sf-1
14e	Human Figurine: Abstract Form, "Stalk" Head Fragment	SI, sf-1
14f	Human Figurine: Abstract Form, "Stalk" Head Fragment	SI, sf-1
14g	Human Figurine: Abstract Form, "Stalk" Head Fragment	SI, sf-1
14h	Human Figurine: Abstract Form, "Stalk" Head Fragment	SI, sf-1
14i	Human Figurine: Abstract Form, "Stalk" Head Fragment	SIw, sf-1
14j	Human Figurine: Abstract Form, "Stalk" Head Fragment	SI, 2
14k	Human Figurine: Abstract Form, "Stalk" Head Fragment	SIc, 2a
14l	Human Figurine: Abstract Form, "Stalk" Head Fragment	SI, sf-1
14m	Human Figurine: Abstract Form, "Stalk" Head Fragment	SIc, 2a
14n	Human Figurine: Abstract Form, "Stalk" Head Fragment	SI, 1a
14o	Human Figurine: Abstract Form, "Stalk" Head Fragment	SI, sf-1
14p	Human Figurine: Miscellaneous Fragment	SI, 3
14q	Human Figurine: Miscellaneous Fragment	SIc, 2a
15a	Abstract Form: "Stalk" Object With "Nail" Head	SI, 3
15b	Abstract Form: "Stalk" Object With "Nail" Head	SI, 3
15c	Abstract Form: "Stalk" Object With "Nail" Head	SIc, 2a
15d	Geometric Form: Cone-Shaped Object	SI, sf-1
15e	Geometric Form: Cone-Shaped Object	SI, 1
15f	Abstract Form: "Stalk" Object With "Nail" Head	SI, sf-1
15g	Abstract Form: "Stalk" Object With "Nail" Head	SI, sf-1
15h	Abstract Form: "Stalk" Object With "Nail" Head	SI, sf-1
15i	Abstract Form: "Stalk" Object With "Nail" Head	SI, sf-1

Catalog 1. Illustrated Figurines and Clay Objects from Sarab—cont.

Plate	*Classification*	*Findspot*
15j	Abstract Form: "Stalk" Object With "Nail" Head	SI, sf-1
15k	Abstract Form: "Stalk" Object With "Nail" Head	SI, 3
15l	Abstract Form: "Stalk" Object With "Nail" Head	SI, sf-1
15m	Abstract Form: "Stalk" Object With "Nail" Head	SIc, 2b
15n	Abstract Form: "Stalk" Object With "Nail" Head	SI, sf-1
15o	Abstract Form: "Stalk" Object With "Nail" Head	SI, sf-1
15p	Abstract Form: Double-Winged-Base Object	SIc, 2
15q	Abstract Form: Double-Winged-Base Object	SI, sf-1
15r	Abstract Form: Double-Winged-Base Object	SI, sf-1
15s	Abstract Form: Double-Winged-Base Object	SIc, 2
15t	Abstract Form: Double-Winged-Base Object	SI, sf-1
15u	Abstract Form: Double-Winged-Base Object	SIc, 2b
15v	Abstract Form: Double-Winged-Base Object	SI, 1a
15w	Abstract Form: Double-Winged-Base Object	SI, sf-1
15x	Abstract Form: Double-Winged-Base Object	SIc, 2
15y	Abstract Form: Double-Winged-Base Object	SIc, 2
15z	Abstract Form: Double-Winged-Base Object	SIc, 2
15aa	Abstract Form: Double-Winged-Base Object	SI, sf-1
15ab	Abstract Form: Double-Winged-Base Object	SI, sf-1
16a	Abstract Form: Stud-Shaped Object	SI, sf-1
16b	Abstract Form: Stud-Shaped Object	SI, 1
16c	Abstract Form: Stud-Shaped Object	SI, sf-1
16d	Abstract Form: Stud-Shaped Object	SI, pit
16e	Abstract Form: Stud-Shaped Object	SI, sf-1
16f	Abstract Form: Stud-Shaped Object	SI, sf-1
16g	Abstract Form: Stud-Shaped Object	SI, 2
16h	Abstract Form: Stud-Shaped Object	SI, sf-1
16i	Geometric Form: Cone-Shaped Object	SI, sf-1
16j	Geometric Form: Cone-Shaped Object	SI, 2
16k	Geometric Form: Cone-Shaped Object	SI, 1+
16l	Geometric Form: Cone-Shaped Object	SI, sf-1
16m	Geometric Form: Cone-Shaped Object	SI, 1j
16n	Geometric Form: Cone-Shaped Object	SI, 1
16o	Geometric Form: Cone-Shaped Object	SIw, sf-1
16p	Geometric Form: Tetrahedron-Shaped Object	SI, sf-1
16q	Geometric Form: Tetrahedron-Shaped Object	SI, sf-1
16r	Geometric Form: Tetrahedron-Shaped Object	SV, 4
16s	Geometric Form: Tetrahedron-Shaped Object	SIc, 2b
16t	Geometric Form: Miscellaneous-Shaped Object	SI, sf-1
17a	Geometric Form: Ball-Shaped Object	SI, sf-1

Catalog 1. Illustrated Figurines and Clay Objects from Sarab—cont.

Plate	*Classification*	*Findspot*
17b	Geometric Form: Ball-Shaped Object	SIw, sf-1
17c	Geometric Form: Ball-Shaped Object	SIw, sf-1
17d	Geometric Form: Flattened Disc-Like Object	SI, 3
17e	Geometric Form: Flattened Disc-Like Object	SI, 2
17f	Geometric Form: Flattened Disc-Like Object	SI, sf-1
17g	Geometric Form: Flattened Disc-Like Object	SI, sf-1
17h	Geometric Form: Rectangular-Shaped Block-Like Object	SI, sf-1
17i	Geometric Form: Rectangular-Shaped Block-Like Object	SIw, 1
17j	Geometric Form: Rectangular-Shaped Block-Like Object	SI, sf-1
17k	Geometric Form: Rectangular-Shaped Block-Like Object	SI, 1
17l	Perforated Form: Bead	SI, sf-1
17m	Perforated Form: Bead	SI, sf-1
17n	Perforated Form: Pendant-Like Bead	SI, sf-1
17o	Perforated Form: Spool-Like Object	SI, sf-1
17p	Perforated Form: Miscellaneous Object	SI, sf-1
17q	Perforated Form: Miscellaneous Object	SI, sf-1
17r	Perforated Form: Miscellaneous Object	SI, sf-1
17s	Perforated Form: Miscellaneous Object	SI, sf-1
17t	Perforated Form: Miscellaneous Object	SI, 1
17u	Perforated Form: Miscellaneous Object	SI, 2a
18a	Miscellaneous Form: Textile Impression on Clay Fragment	SI, 2a
18b	Miscellaneous Form: Textile Impression on Clay Fragment	SI, 2b
18c	Miscellaneous Form: Textile Impression on Clay Fragment	SI, sf-1
18d	Miscellaneous Form: Twill Matting Impression on Clay Fragment	SI, sf-1
18e	Miscellaneous Form: Twill Matting Impression on Clay Fragment	SI, 3
18f	Miscellaneous Form: Twill Matting Impression on Clay Fragment (Positive of 18e)	
18g	Miscellaneous Form: Split-Reed Basket or Mat Impression on Clay Fragment	SI, 2b
18h	Miscellaneous Form: Basket Impression on Clay Fragment	SIc, 2
18i	Miscellaneous Form: Basket Impression on Clay Fragment (Positive of 18h)	
18j	Miscellaneous Form: Twill Matting Impression on Clay Fragment	SIc, 2aj

Sarab—Animal Figurines: Curly-Tailed Dogs. Scale 1:1.

Sarab—Animal Figurines: Wild Pigs. Scale 1:1.

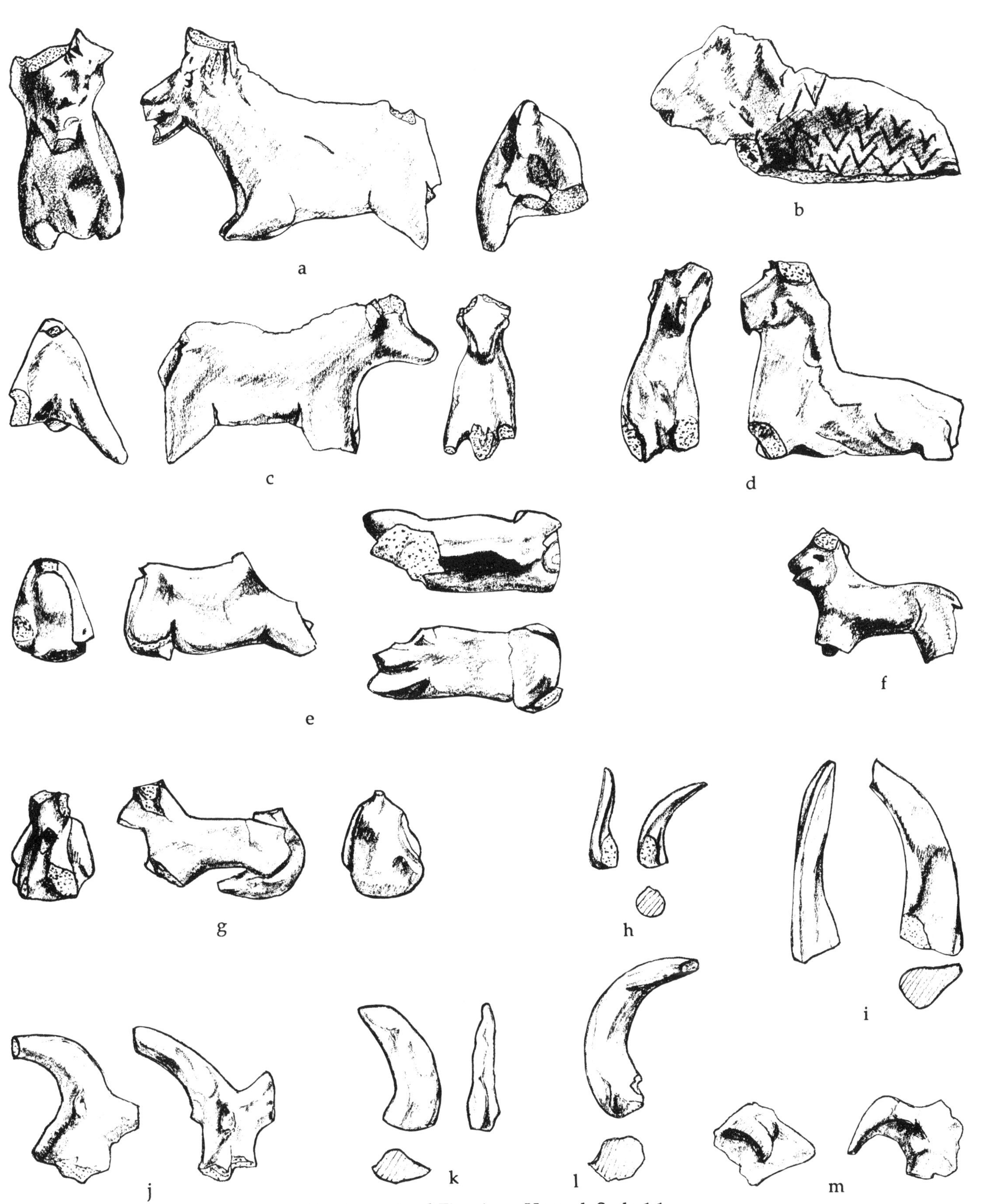

Sarab—Animal Figurines: Horned. Scale 1:1.

Plate 4

Sarab—Animal Figurines: (*a-c*) With Tails Up, (*d-k*) With Tails Out, and (*l-o*) With Tails Down. Scale 1:1.

Sarab—Animal Figurines: Non-Classifiable Fragments. Scale 1:1.

Plate 6

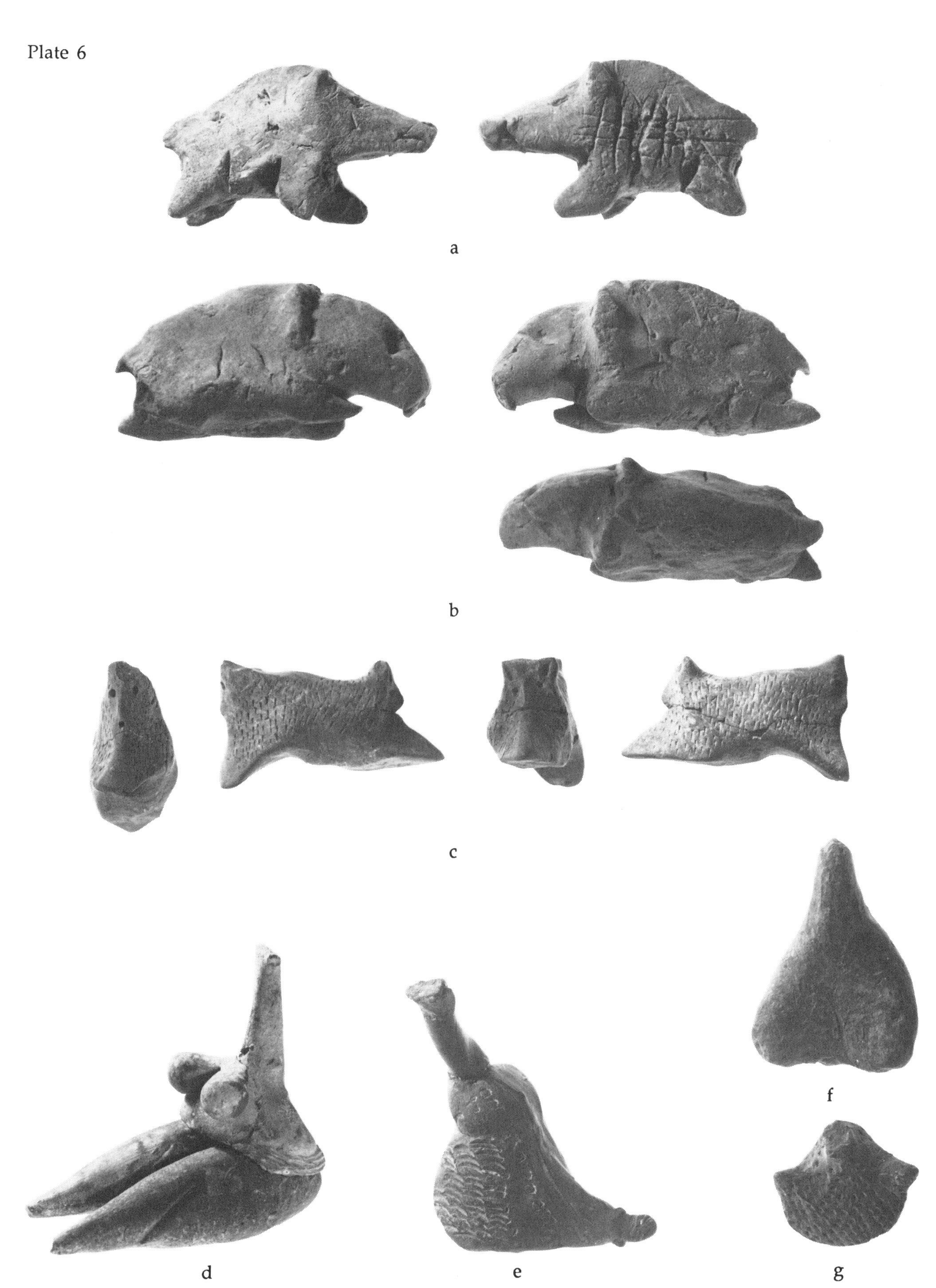

Sarab—Animal and Human Figurines: (*a, b*) Wild Pigs, (*c*) Non-Classifiable Fragment, Animal, (*d*) Composite Form, Human Female, (*e*) Abstract Form, Human "Snail Lady," and (*f, g*) Miscellaneous Fragments, Human. Scale 1:1.

Plate 7

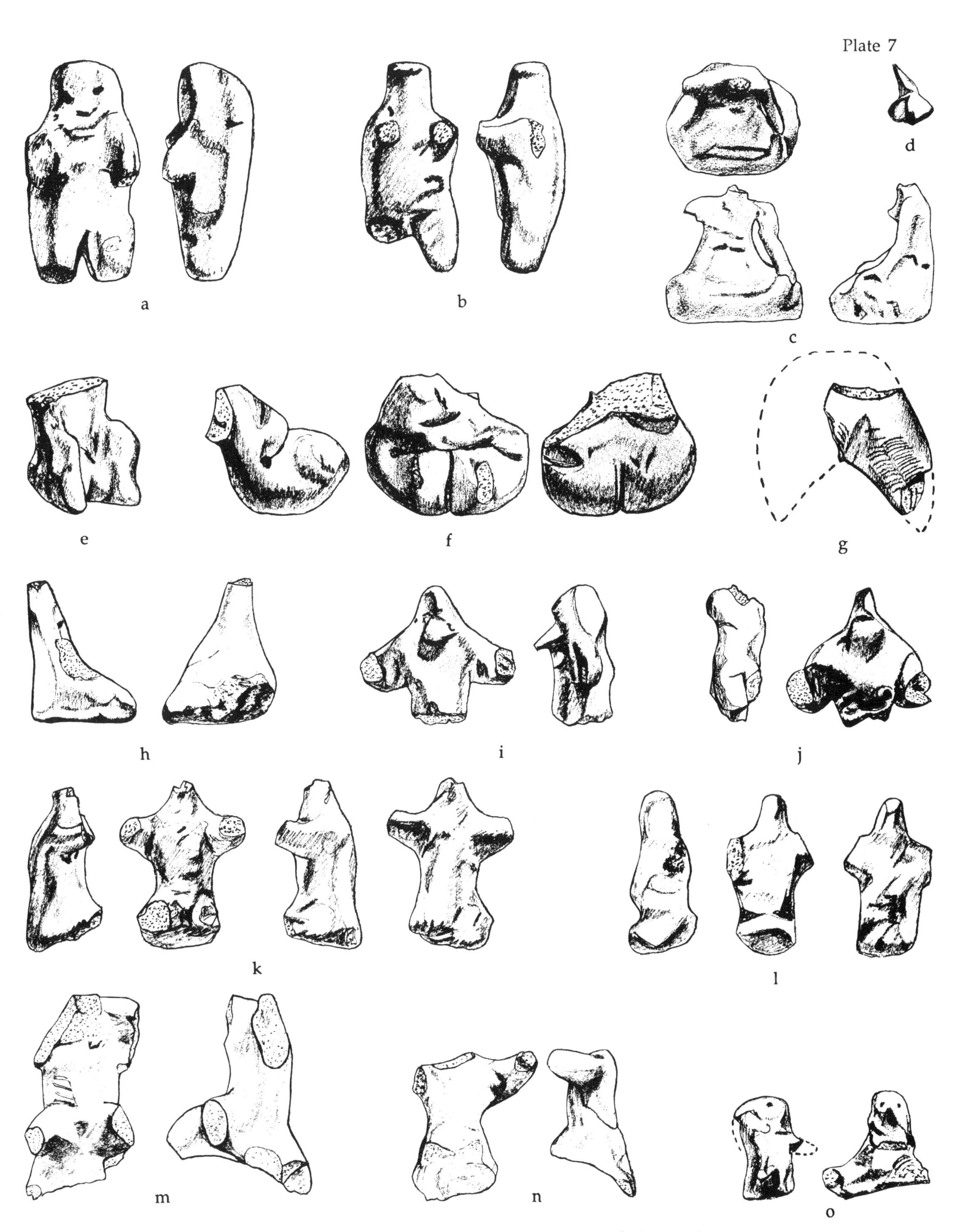

Sarab—Human Figurines: (*a, b*) Simple Extended Forms, (*c-h*) Simple Seated Forms, and (*i-o*) Male Torsos with Extended Arms. Scale 1:1.

Plate 8

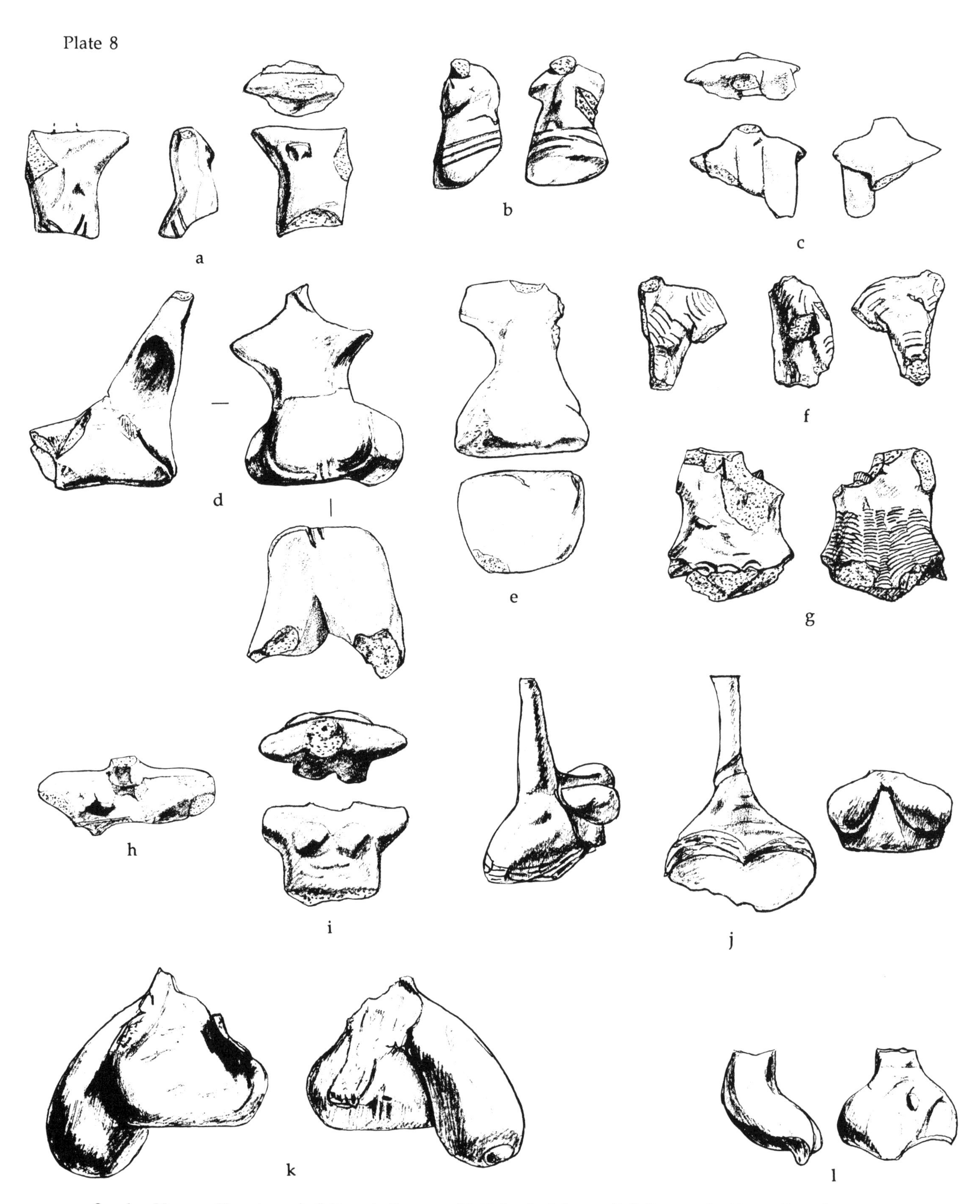

Sarab—Human Figurines: (*a-i*) Female Torsos with Extended Arms, (*j, l*) Composite Form, Female Torso Fragments, and (*k*) Composite Form, Female Breast Fragment. Scale 1:1.

Sarab—Human Figurines: (*a, b, f,* and *g*) Composite Form, Female Torso Fragments and (*c-e* and *h*) Composite Form, Female Breast Fragments. Scale 1:1.

Plate 10

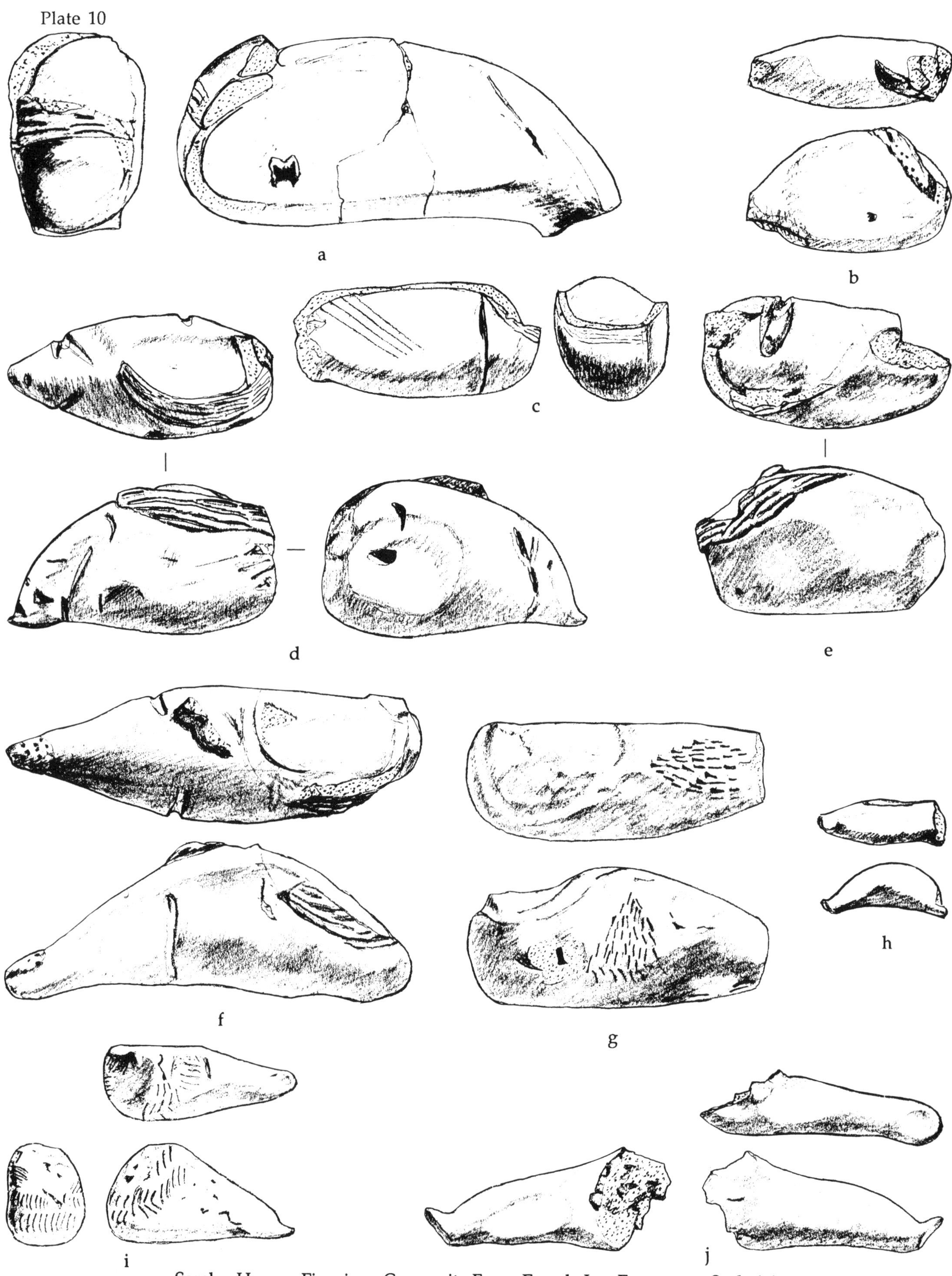

Sarab—Human Figurines: Composite Form, Female Leg Fragments. Scale 1:1.

Plate 11

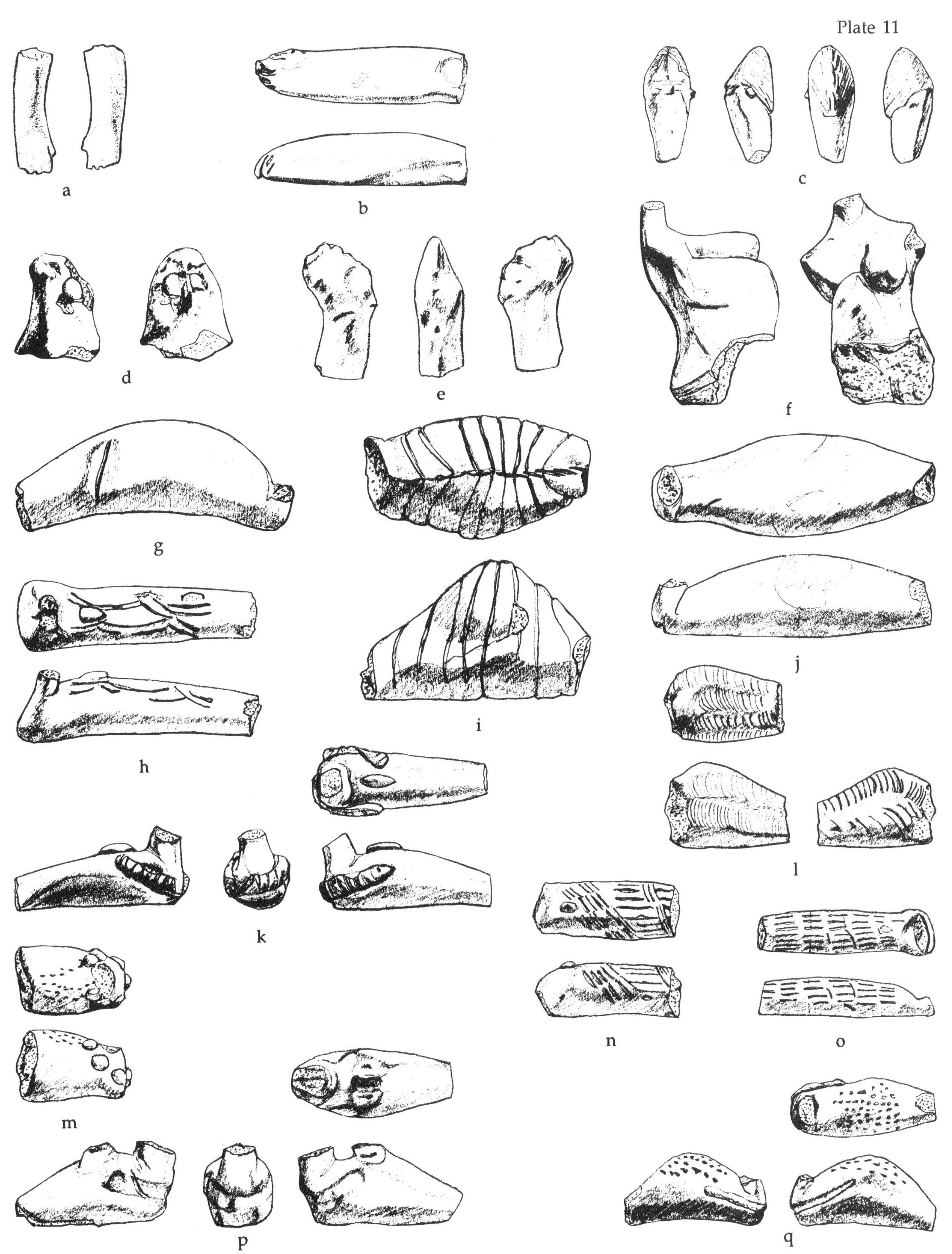

Sarab—Human Figurines: (*a*, *b*) Composite Form, Arm Fragments, (*c-e*) Composite Form, Head Fragments, and (*f-q*) Abstract Form, "Lady Stalk" Fragments. Scale 1:1.

Plate 12

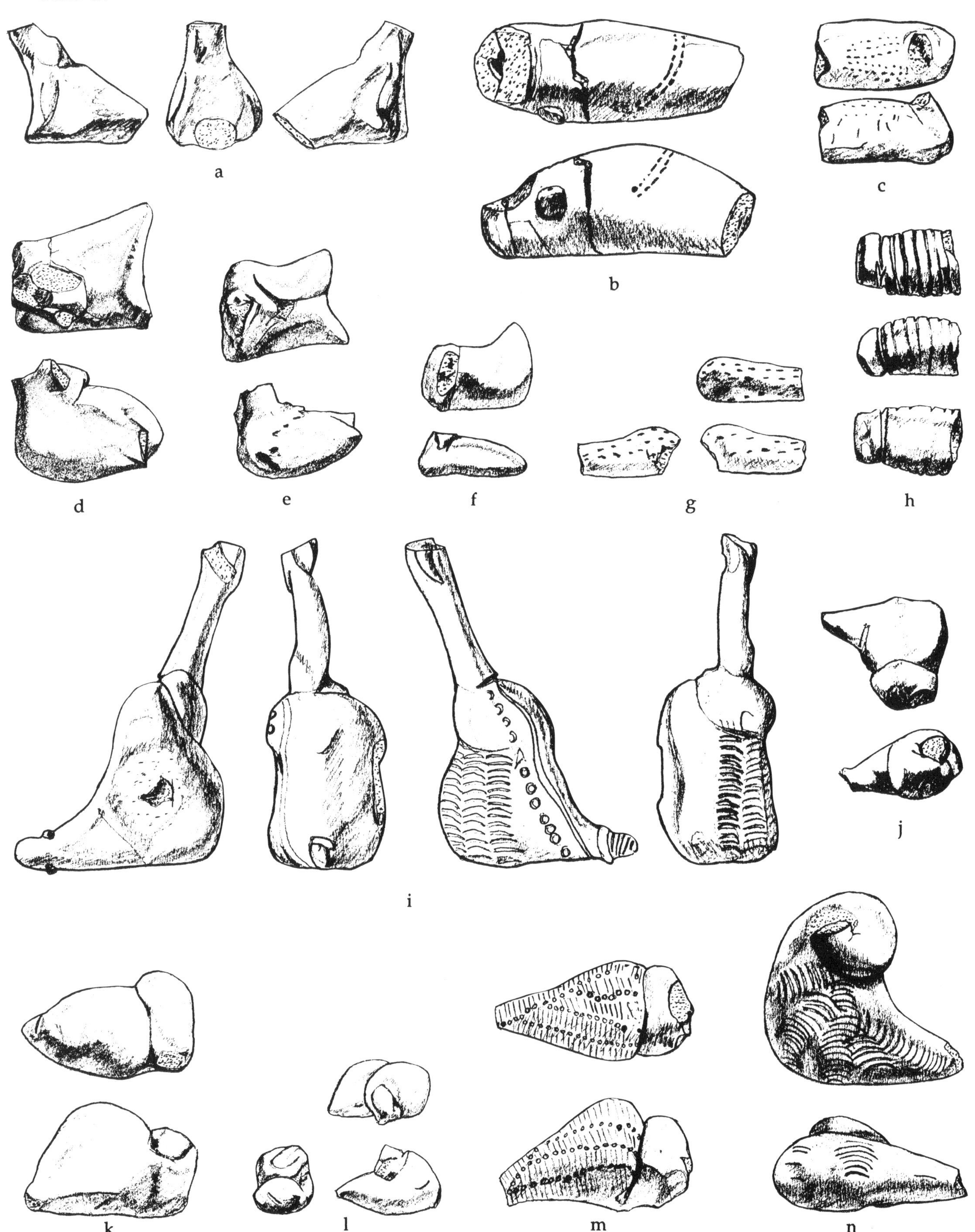

Sarab—Human Figurines: (*a-h*) Abstract Form, "Lady Stalk" Fragments and (*i*) Abstract Form, "Snail Lady," and (*j-n*) Fragments of "Snail Ladies." Scale 1:1.

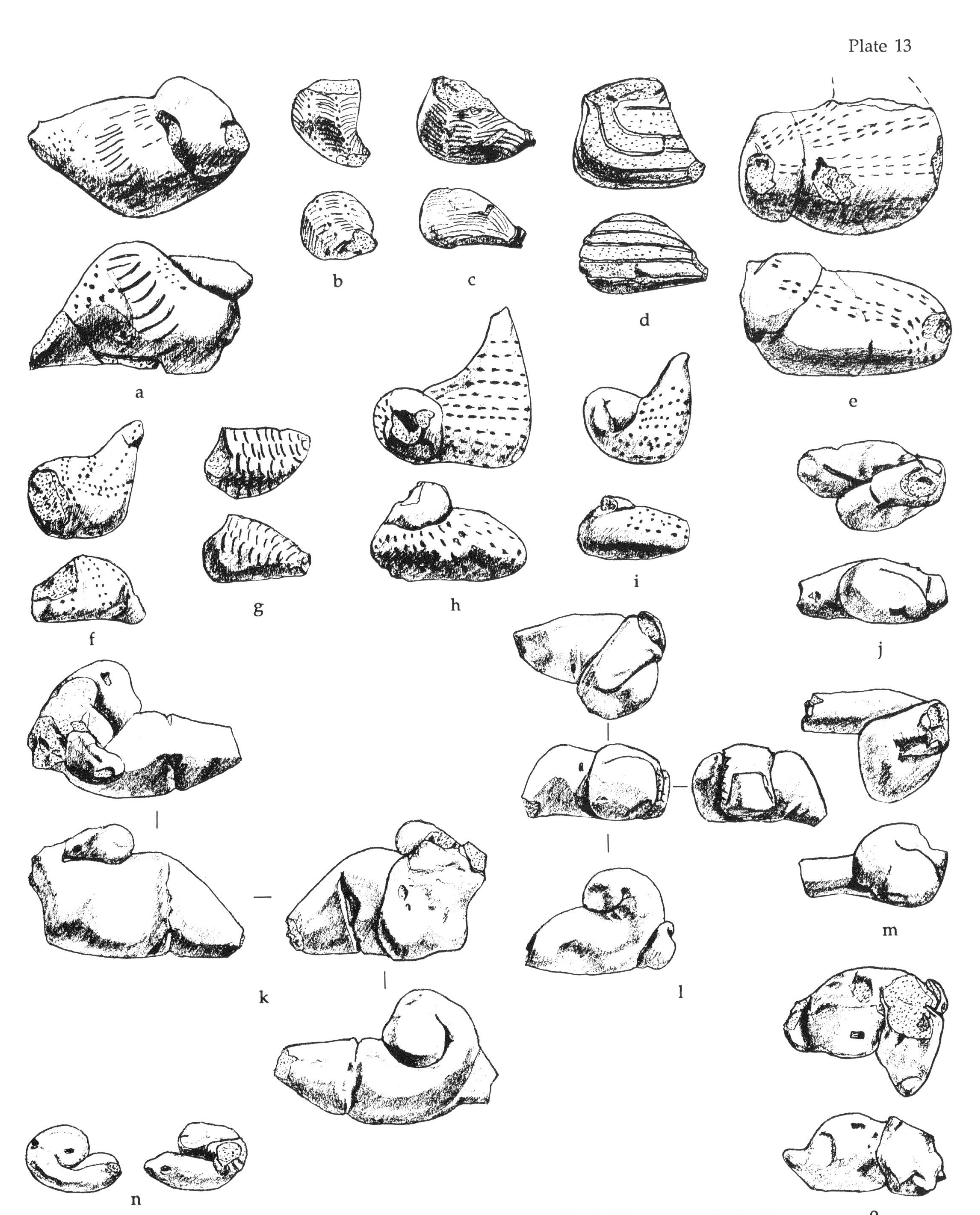

Sarab—Human Figurines: Abstract Form, "Snail Lady" Fragments. Scale 1:1.

Plate 14

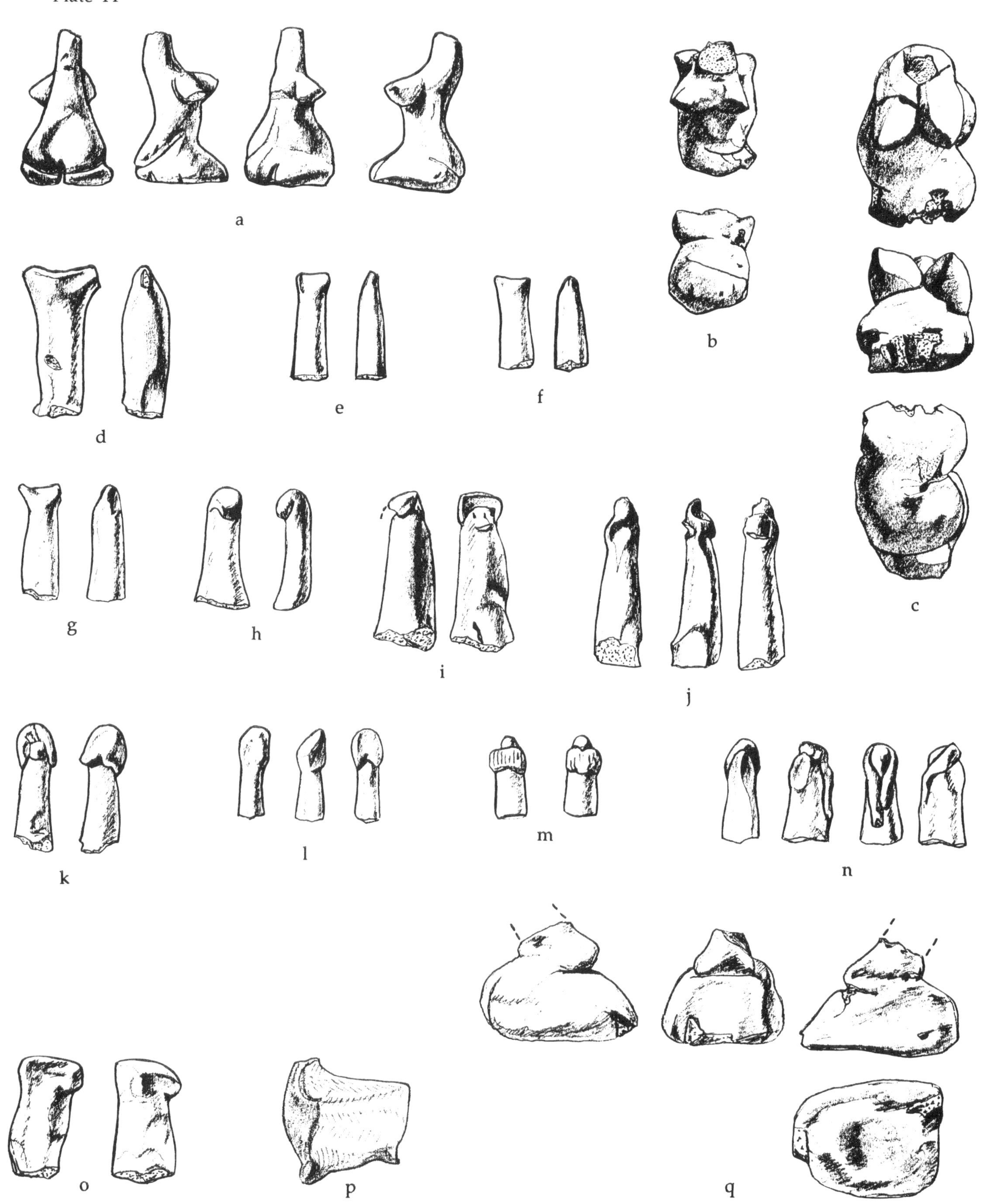

Sarab—Human Figurines: (*a-c*) Abstract Form, "Snail Lady" Fragments, (*d-o*) Abstract Form, "Stalk" Head Fragments, and (*p, q*) Miscellaneous Fragments. Scale 1:1.

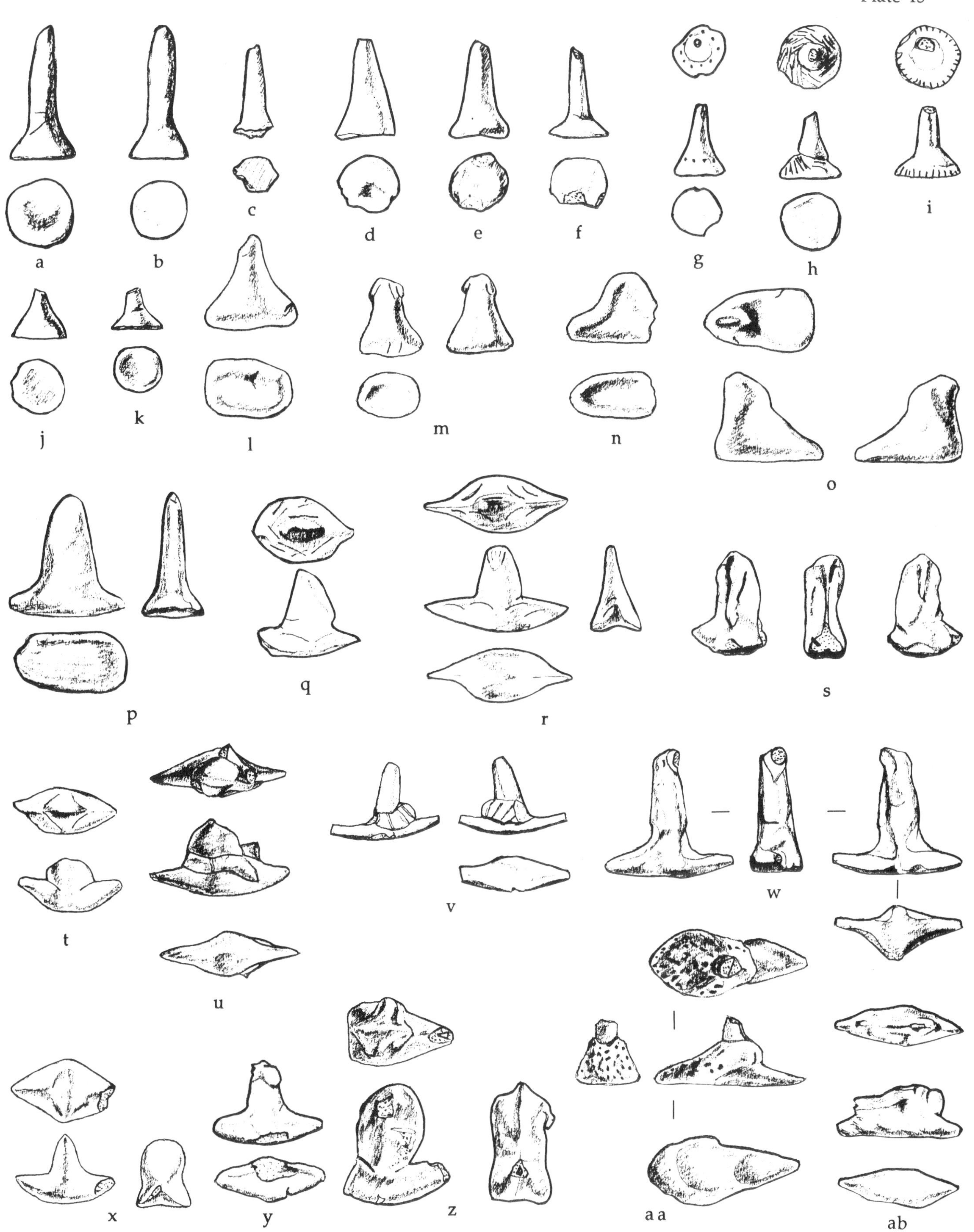

Sarab—Abstract and Geometric Forms: (*a-c* and *f-o*) Abstract "Stalk" Objects with "Nail" Heads, (*d, e*) Geometric Cone-Shaped Objects, and (*p-ab*) Abstract Double-Winged-Base Objects. Scale 1:1.

Plate 16

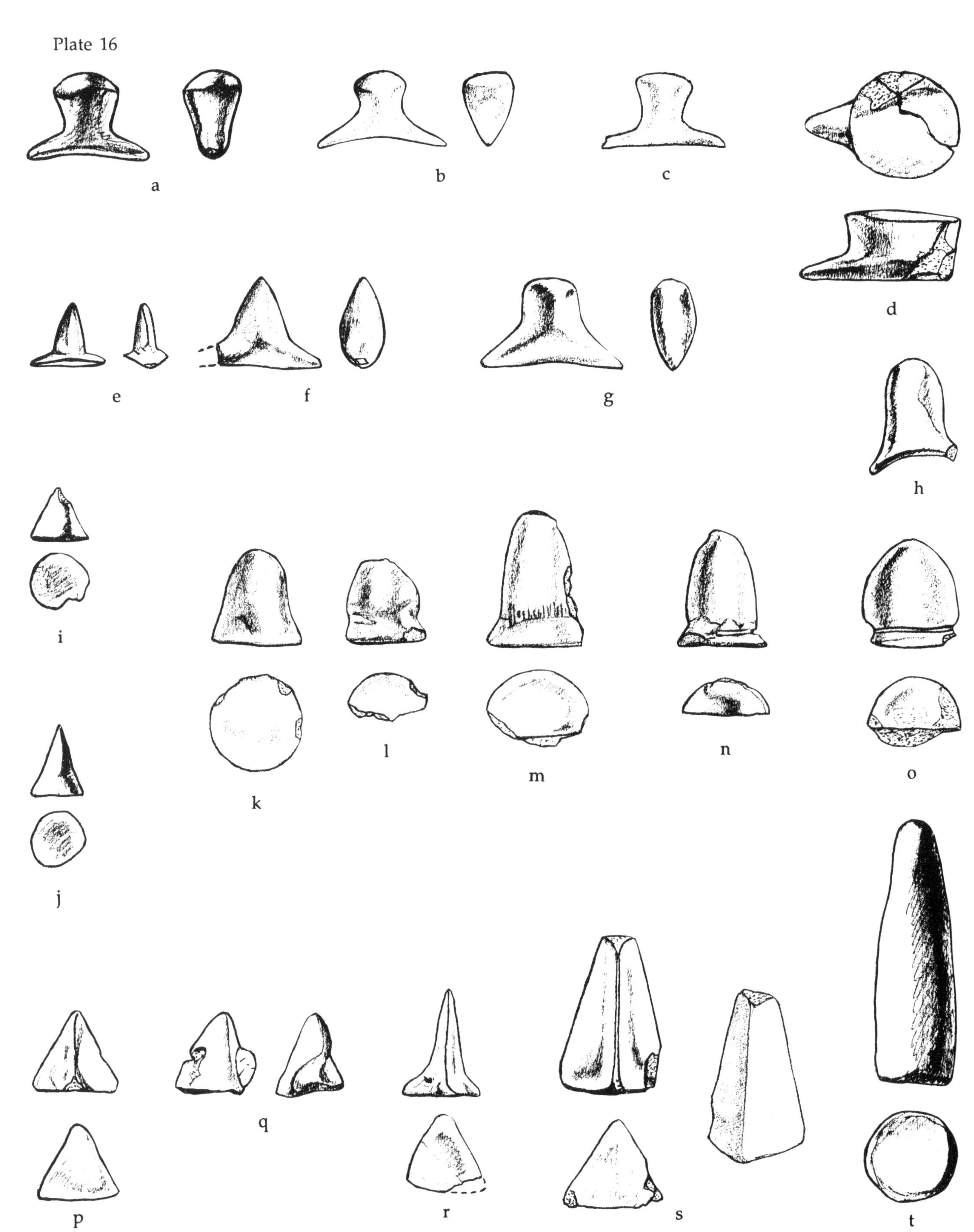

Sarab—Abstract and Geometric Forms: (*a-h*) Abstract Stud-Shaped Objects, (*i-o*) Geometric Cone-Shaped Objects, (*p-s*) Geometric Tetrahedron-Shaped Objects, and (*t*) Geometric Miscellaneous-Shaped Object. Scale 1:1.

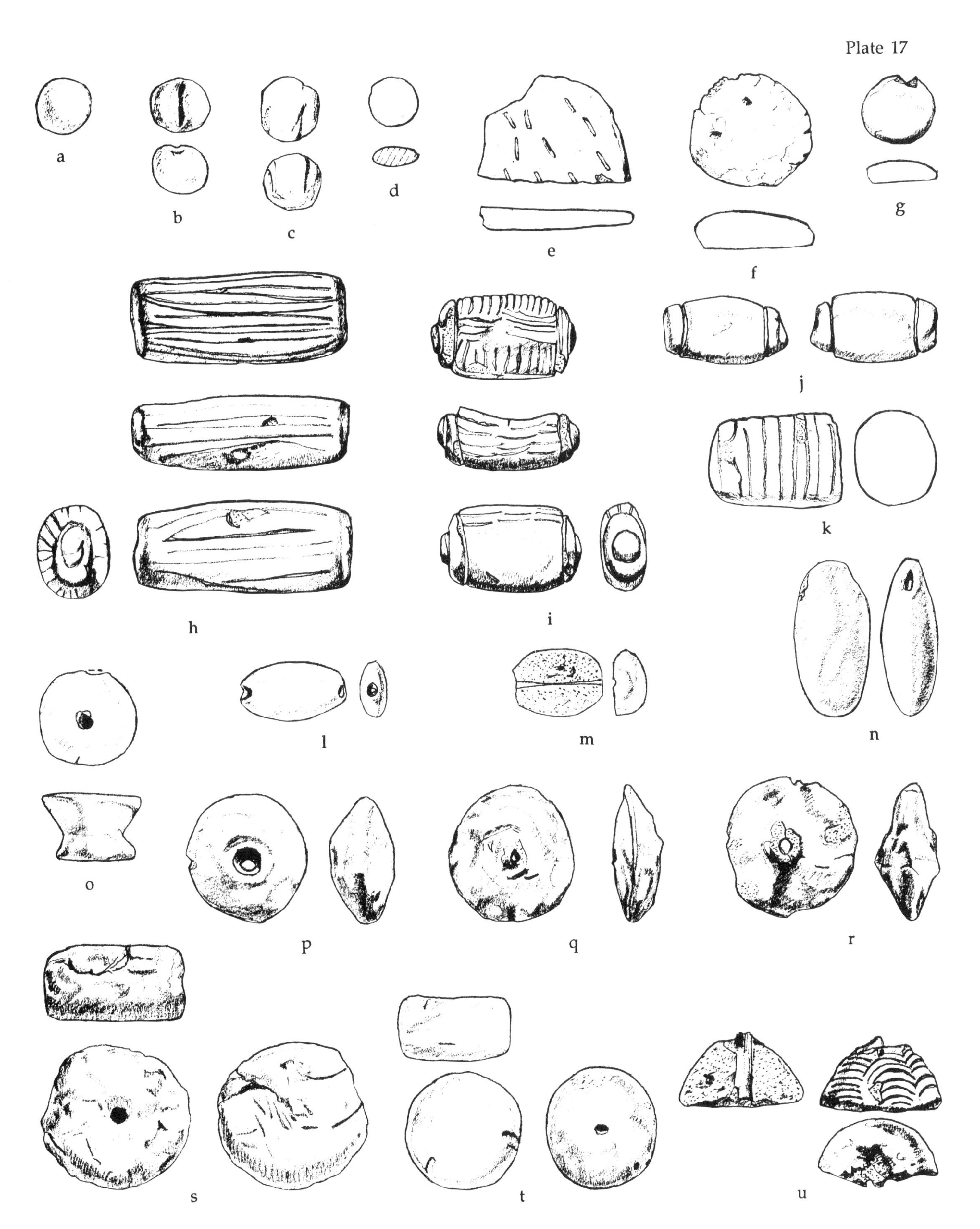

Sarab—Geometric and Perforated Forms: (*a-c*) Geometric Ball-Shaped Objects, (*d-g*) Geometric Flattened Disc-Like Objects, (*h-k*) Geometric Rectangular-Shaped Block-Like Objects, (*l*, *m*) Perforated Beads, (*n*) Perforated Pendant-Like Bead, (*o*) Perforated Spool-Like Object, and (*p-u*) Perforated Miscellaneous Objects. Scale 1:1.

Plate 18

Sarab—Miscellaneous Forms: (*a-c*) Textile Impressions on Clay Fragments, (*d, e*) Twill Matting Impressions on Clay Fragments, (*f*) Positive Impression of *e*, (*g*) Split-Reed Basket or Mat Impression on Clay Fragment, (*h, j*) Basket Impression on Clay Fragments, and (*i*) Positive Impression of *h*. Scale 2:1, except *a* 1:1.

FIGURINES AND OTHER CLAY OBJECTS FROM ÇAYÖNÜ

INTRODUCTION

The clay figurine material through the 1987 season at Çayönü consists of about 400 pieces. This collection may seem surprisingly small given the number of field seasons devoted to excavation there, but the soil conditions prevailing at the site almost precluded the finding any clay objects at all. The soil is very compacted and clayey, which made careful pick-work extremely slow going. The obligatory smashing of the lumps of consolidated earth resulted in poor preservation of those tiny fragments, which were found in the houses or in the debris outside of the dwellings, that had already broken in antiquity. Flotation, while excellent for the recovery of seeds and carbon, is not useful for the recovery of small objects of lightly baked clay, because water tends to dissolve them.

Certain areas of the mound were also disturbed by habitation in later times when pits were dug down into the earlier levels. An area to the northeast has been found to contain pottery and overlies pre-ceramic levels. The early architecture is well preserved due to the compacted soil, so that recovered clay material from undisturbed early levels has good provenience. Where the provenience is not clear, the piece is noted as contextless (i.e., "surface" or "surface-l").

Distribution appears to be general. Only in the structural remains first called SA (1968 and 1972) and U (1970) are there numbers of figurine fragments. (U 9 is the burned house where the two house models were found.) Figurines were more often found within houses than in open areas without construction.

The types of clay used in the manufacture of the objects described here would seem to be available locally. Some of the pieces have pebble inclusions which weakened the fabric and caused breaks, both old and new. Chaff or other organic material was also sometimes mixed with the wet clay; this burned out in the baking of the object. Other pieces, and these are usually small and well modeled, were made of fine-grained clay, probably that which silted out naturally down along the river banks.

The objects were then baked; it appears from fragments freshly broken that at Çayönü the figurines were fairly well fired. They certainly seem to be quite hard on the surface. Some were further baked in the burning of the houses in which they were found.

The colors range through all of the buffs; grayish, yellowish, and reddish. There are many which are brick-red. Cores in these small objects are generally the same color as the surface, although blackened cores do occur. As at Jarmo and Sarab (Broman Morales 1983:393, n. 1; and p. 10, above), the clay figurines were deliberately fired after manufacture, which insured a short term existence but did not constitute a preparation for permanence.

Permanence could have been obtained by the manufacture of figurines in stone. Bowls, bracelets, and beads attest to the skill of the Çayönü inhabitants in working stone. But there is only one example (and none at Jarmo or Sarab) of a small figurine of stone. A banded pink and white limestone pebble has been used and the figure is female (pl. 25a). It is a torso form with rounded knob head, arms akimbo, and rather long, large breasts that are placed wide apart on the chest. The pebble is waisted and the back and buttocks show the swirls of the banding to advantage.

Of the miscellaneous forms included in the clay material at Çayönü, three forms are unusually large. One is that of the house models; these were constructed of sticks and chaff-tempered mud that was used in building. Then there are six clay basins that were obviously utilitarian. The final form is that of pestle-shaped objects. These pieces will be described in the final pages of this report, however, since they are made of clay and there are too few of them to be presented in the reports of other artifacts.

The drawings of all the pieces are at 1:1 scale. The shallow basins are at 1:2 scale.

The three major categories are those of the animal figurines, human figurines, and geometric forms. The totals are fifty, seventy-five, and one hundred twenty-five respectively, which comprise a little more than half of the pieces in the collection.

The classification of the clay figurine material at Çayönü is based on the study of the larger collections of Jarmo in Iraq and Sarab in Iran. Without this base of approximately 7,500 fragments it would have been very difficult to work with such a small number of pieces. The interpretation of the possible use or meaning of these clay objects also derives from the study of the Jarmo and Sarab material. The figurines from these early sites are considered to be magic wish-figures.

ANIMAL FIGURINES

Of the major categories there are fewer examples of animal figurines. This is puzzling in view of the fact that quantities of animal bone were found throughout all levels of the site. Dog was present (Lawrence 1980:301-303) as the only domesticated animal in the earliest levels. Wild pig was hunted, probably with the aid of the dogs, and wild sheep and goats also were hunted, as well as wild cattle and deer. The domestication of sheep (and possibly of goats) has been determined for the upper levels (Lawrence 1982:190).

Two factors could help to account for the scarcity of animal wish-figures in clay. The first is that of preservation and recovery, which were difficult in most of the areas excavated, and the second would perhaps be that of abundance. A hunter might well have been able to secure a wild animal with relative ease not too far from the settlement, especially in the earlier periods.

HORNED ANIMALS (pls. 19 and 20a-f) — 12 examples

Only one of the twelve examples of horned animal figurines is not a sheep or a goat and looks very much like a cow. This piece has a flat base and suggests an animal lying down. The horns, now broken off, projected straight out from the sides of the head (pl. 19a). Since there is as yet no evidence that bovines were domesticated at this time, this figure would represent a wild form.

Another horned animal has its horns broken off on the sides of the head which would indicate that they extended out and forward (pl. 19f). The two other more or less whole figurines (one illustrated on pl. 19e) perhaps were meant to represent goats, while the two bodies without heads and thus without an indication of horns are perhaps meant to represent in turn a goat with a short tail turned up (pl. 20b) and a sheep with a short tail turned down and pressed against the back (pl. 20c). Another piece, the head and forepart only, was terminated mid-section by pinching off the plastic clay and left a rounded surface (pl. 19b). This example seems to have had horns that were broken off and is the only figurine of this type that has a pinched spine; it could represent either sheep or goat.

There are two figurines that look very much like sheep. One is quite small and has no trace of horns (pl. 20a). It could depict a female domesticated sheep since the female loses its horns when domesticated. Unfortunately, this piece comes from a disturbed area where much later material in association with pottery obscures the stratigraphy. The second figure is unusual in that it stands on an oval base that is concave (pl. 19c). The body is smooth and rounded and the head is held high on a long neck. There are old and worn breaks on the back and sides of the head so that it is not clear whether or not this piece had horns. It looks like a reclining animal that is alert with its head up.

A headless body fragment may represent a sheep. This piece has a smoothly rounded back, a small fold between the front legs, and a broad back end with a short turned-down tab tail. There are two heads; one, with the nose and both horns broken off close to the head, may represent a goat (pl. 20d). The other is larger with horns that project out from the sides of the head (pl. 19d). The horns are broken off. The nose is round and blunt at the tip. This piece resembles the first horned animal figure described as bovine (pl. 19a).

There are eight horns, two of which are illustrated (pl. 20e, f); both are keeled by pinching and would therefore have come from figurines representing goats, since sheep horns are round in section. The remaining six horns have round sections.

CURLY-TAILED DOGS (pl. 20g-i) 3 examples

Domesticated dogs were certainly present at Çayönü as well as at Jarmo (Lawrence 1980:301-303; Lawrence and Reed 1983:485-494). It would therefore be logical to find figurines of dogs. Curly-tailed dogs are known in the figurine material of Jarmo and Sarab. The distinguishing feature here is the tail; only the dog has a tail that curves up and over the back.

There are only three figurines at Çayönü that may represent dogs. The first piece is headless with a massive forepart tapering to the back. The tail is curled around and pressed to the right flank (pl. 20h). The next example is a more or less whole figure that is well modeled with a rounded back (pl. 20i). The tail is broken off and the break is worn, but a suggestion of a curl remains. There is an indentation on top of the back where the tail could have been pressed down. The last piece is a hind end fragment; the tail, although broken off, is shown in an upright position (pl. 20g).

WILD PIGS (pl. 21a, b) 5 examples

The characteristics of the wild pig as modeled in clay have been established in the study of the collections of Jarmo and Sarab. The spine is pinched up along the back and forms a crest over the head. The nose is long and pointed while the body is heavy in front and tapers to the rear. Five examples at Çayönü appear to represent the pig. One is only a head and forepart with a long pointed snout and a high crest pinched up over the head (pl. 21b), two more or less whole figurines have a pinched spine (e.g., pl. 21a), and the last two are body fragments that have a pinched spine.

NON-CLASSIFIABLE (pl. 21c-f) 22 examples

Two almost whole figurines have indications of long thick tails that extend straight out behind (pl. 21c, d). Two headless examples have thick extended tails that are broken off. Two others are hind end fragments. These six are non-classifiable as to the animal they represent. Two other figurines seem to have carried a burden (or a rider?) as there are lumps of clay or depressions for appliqué on top of the back (e.g., pl. 21e). Another more or less whole figurine has a pointed nose, erect ears, short legs, and an elongated body with a smooth back (pl. 21f). The tail position is difficult to establish; it may have been like the one illustrated on plate 21c, or it may have been turned up. In addition there is a forepart fragment and five body mid-sections that are too fragmentary to be classified, as well as seven legs of a shape and size consistent with those of the animal figurines.

DISCUSSION

One interpretation of clay animal figurines in early settlements is that they were made with the hope of attracting specific animals in the hunt, a kind of wish-magic that went into the plastic clay as it was formed. These wish figures were probably discarded casually after the hunt was over, which thereby accounted for their presence throughout the habitation areas. They were not created as permanent objects and so were not considered important. With the exception of the dog, the animal figurines at Çayönü undoubtedly refer mainly to wild and therefore hunted animals, at least in the earliest levels.

In general, the modeling of the animal figurines of Çayönü is not very well done. No example was found, for instance, that could have carried the beautifully shaped goat horn illustrated on plate 20e. Perhaps the abundance of wild game close at hand did not stimulate the production of animal figures.

HUMAN FIGURINES

This category has four basic forms in the Çayönü material: the simple seated female, the related lady stalk, the composite female, and the torso form. There are in addition one head and some fragments that cannot be classified.

SIMPLE SEATED FORM (pl. 22a, c-f, h) — 14 examples

The simple seated female is basically a cone with legs added or pulled out from the base. There are fourteen examples, only three of which are more or less whole. These three have stalk heads with no modification for features; two of the stalk tips are pointed and one is rounded. This last is a small example (pl. 22a), which is a bright red-orange in color with a very hard and smooth surface. There is a stomach appliquéd over the legs. There may have been tiny breasts appliquéd above the stomach, but this is not clear as the piece is very small. In any case, this figure is the only one with a stomach and therefore perhaps represents a pregnant female.

The other two whole figurines sit very well. Instead of having buttocks, one has a short leg-like projection in back to make it stable (pl. 22c). The other figurine is beautifully fashioned (pl. 22d). Conical in shape, it has short plump legs with rounded tips. The buttocks are delineated and buttressed on the sides by modeling. All of the other figurines of this type have rounded backs.

One of these with very short stumpy legs has appliquéd pellets around the waist (pl. 22e). There are four pellets in place and depressions indicate that there were at least four more. The appliqué seems to represent a belt or sash. The cylindrical stalk is thick and rises straight up to a break. This piece is nicely modeled and well shaped. Another very similar piece is missing the left leg and has no decoration.

A variation of these last two figurines has the right leg extended forward, while the left leg seems to be coiled into the body (pl. 22f). The coil is not very evident, but there is no break where an extended leg might have broken off. The stalk body is cylindrical and broken off mid-way. There is a pebble inclusion at the break which weakens the fabric at this point.

A whole base with the cylindrical stalk broken off has two plump and rounded legs. These legs look rather like breasts but are probably not since the base is flat and finished.

Finally, there are seven fragments that seem to be related to the others since they retain the basic shape of a triangle (e.g., pl. 22h). They have projecting legs of which one is at least partial while the other one is broken off close to the body. To conclude, this simple seated form is an abstract one.

LADY STALKS—ABSTRACT FORM (pls. 22b, g, i and 23a-c) 20 examples

The next form is that of the lady stalk (as at Sarab see p. 15 above, and for Jarmo, Broman Morales 1983:380f.). This differs from the first form in that the projecting legs are modeled as one. There are twenty examples of this type which represents an abstraction of the seated female. Nine of the figurines have the top of the stalk broken off. The first of the more or less whole examples could be considered a transition between the simple seated form and the lady stalk. The cylindrical stalk ends in a rounded top, while the bottom part is pulled out to produce a flat circular base. Thin curved legs are appliquéd on top of the base, the left side of which has been broken off at the edge (pl. 22b). A similar whole figurine has the base projecting to a point while the top is rounded and pinched (pl. 22g). A less well shaped piece has an oval base with a tiny pointed projection that represents the legs. The tapered stalk ends in a rounded top (pl. 22i). Another piece has short rounded arms which extend out from the sides just below the rounded stump head. The flat base comes to a blunt rounded end in front. A deep diagonal perforation is probably meant to represent the umbilicus (pl. 23a).

A piece with a vertically flattened stalk ends in a top pinched out to a rounded point behind and a pinched out "nose" (broken off) in front (pl. 23b). The projecting leg ends in a rounded point. This piece resembles the double-winged-base figurines of Jarmo in its upper part. Eleven of the remaining pieces are wedge-shaped with the leg or leg end broken off; the stalk of eight of them is also broken off. One of these has had the stalk folded down over the leg to form the stomach and this is separated from the leg by a horizontal incision. There are slight depressions on either side of the stalk where breasts may have been appliquéd. The tip of the leg comes to a point. The bottom part of the base has been sheared off.

One piece with the stalk that ends in a rounded top has a piece of an appliquéd strip on the right side of the stalk. The bottom is flat and there is no modeling of the buttocks; the back is rounded. Another figurine, whose head ends in a pointed rather than a rounded top, has the buttocks separated from the back by modeling. The leg is broken off.

The last piece of the eleven was already in the Diyarbakir museum when this study was being completed, but a scale drawing shows that it had a flattened cylindrical top. A depression around the waist shows where an appliquéd strip had been pressed on. The back is rounded.

Three tall cylindrical stalk fragments with flattened tops are smooth and well shaped. The leg ends are broken off; on one example it would appear that the leg coiled around to one side.

Two figurines are included here although they have no projecting leg. One is basically a stalk (the top is broken off) with a slightly protruding stomach. Breasts were appliquéd, but only the left one remains. Prominent buttocks also seem to have been added (pl. 23c). The other figurine is very lumpy and the breaks are old and worn.

COMPOSITE FORM (pls. 23d-g) 7 examples

The composite female figurine at Çayönü is represented by four body fragments and three legs. This type of figurine is composed of a central body core, usually conical in shape, to which extended paired legs are applied to produce a seated figure. Arms, breasts, and a loin cloth or g-string may also be added to this core. The stalk terminates in a simple rounded top or a more realistically modeled head may be formed.

In the Jarmo and Sarab collections, a hole often was left on the flattened inner surface of the paired legs. This was due to the use of a short straw or tiny stick to dowel the legs and hold them together while shaping the figurine. This stick burned out in the firing or disintegrated with time.

The best example of this type (pl. 23d) sits tilting back with the stalk ending in a rounded point. Rounded breasts (the left one is broken off) were added to the body cone. Fat rounded legs in a bent knee position were added to make a figure that sits well. Although the right leg and the front part of the left one have been broken off, this figurine is easily reconstructed.

One of the body fragments found at Çayönü consists of the stalk section with the top broken off, a rod-like right leg with the end missing, and the left leg entirely broken off (pl. 23f). The buttocks are indicated and a broad appliquéd strip across the top of the legs ends on either side. Another body fragment consists of only a part of a stalk body with appliquéd breasts still adhering. The back of the stalk fragment has been sheared off. There is one small figurine fragment consisting of the left half of a base; the leg ends in a broad rounded point. There is a perforation on the inner side of the fragment and a depression around the waist in back shows where an appliquéd strip has broken off.

The three legs belonging to this type are as follows: The more or less whole leg (pl. 23e) has a flattened base. It is also flattened on one side, which indicates that another leg was pressed next to it. The leg tapers to a point and is round in section. A strip of appliqué remains at the top and outside of the leg, which shows where it was joined to the body and indicates that this was the right leg. There is also a small flat round pellet adhering to the top of the leg.

The other leg is nicely modeled, but the foot end is missing; the flattened inner surface shows that this is the left leg. The body is broken off, but a rim of clay shows how the join was smoothed over. The top of the leg exhibits a smooth and rounded surface (pl. 23g).

The last piece has been broken at the foot end. The back of the leg is battered and worn. The inner surface is flattened, which shows this to have been a left leg. On top a slight rim of clay indicates where the body was attached. The bottom of the leg is flattened at the back end so that the front of the leg was slightly lifted when the figure was whole.

TORSOS AND BASES (pl. 24) 19 examples

The last form in the human figurine category is that of the torso which seems to represent a standing figure. Instead of modeling the legs, the maker formed a torso that ends in a more or less round base which is flat or slightly concave on the bottom. (This form is most clearly seen in the Jarmo figurine collection where there are about 100 examples [Broman Morales 1983, fig. 161]. It is also present at Sarab, see pl. 7i-o.) In these other collections, the torso figurines had a massive back and chest and extended arms, most often in a curved embracing position; I am assuming that this particular torso form represents a male figure.

Of the eleven examples with arms at Çayönü, only one shows this embracing position (pl. 24a). This figure has a vertically pinched head that is rounded on top. It does not appear that there were any features. One other has arms stretched out to the sides (pl. 24b). Three others have only rounded stumps to suggest arms (e.g., pl. 24c, d), while there are two with appliquéd strips folded across the chest to represent arms (pl. 24e, g). These last also have pinched noses to form the face; on one there are round pellets appliquéd for eyes. The top of the head is broken off but probably ended in a rounded tip. The other example is smaller and cruder but is whole and may have had pellet eyes. It is roughly fashioned and ends in a round, slightly concave base. The head is rounded.

Of the fragments included in this group of torsos, one body mid-section is tentatively classified here (pl. 24f). The back is very flat and there seem to have been two pellets appliquéd on the front (to represent breasts?). Also, three arms are tentatively classified with the torso form.

The maleness of the Çayönü torso is in doubt. The massive back and chest and the all-embracing arms are not evident here. The possibility that one piece, although tentatively classified, had breasts requires a different assessment of the sex of these torso figures. It would be necessary to have several more examples to be able to resolve this problem.

Four more or less whole examples are related to the torso form. The first one has a flat-topped, elongated head without features, appliquéd arms pressed to the chest, and an elongated body that terminates in short stumpy legs (pl. 24h). The buttocks are very low on the body. The figure at present does not seem to have been seated, but a piece broken off the lower back and base may originally have created a seated figure. A similar figurine has no arms and the top of the head is slightly concave. Except for the tiny legs and the possible seated position, these first two figurines suggest the torso type.

The other two figurines, one rather crude and roughly fashioned and one smaller and more carefully made, have wide spread legs (pl. 24i, j). Since they neither stand nor sit, they suggest riders, which perhaps are to be mounted on an animal figurine (e.g., pl. 21e). The cruder one has a rounded head, no features, and appliquéd pellet arms pressed onto the sides. The legs end in rounded points and the buttocks are shaped and rounded. The smaller, more carefully made figure has a round, flat-topped head; the arms are short, pointed, and extend out to the sides. The legs are long and thin; the right leg partially is broken off, while the left leg ends in a rounded point with a flap of clay that delineates the foot.

Finally there are nine fragments that may represent human forms, but they are non-classifiable. All are fairly small but differ enough from the examples in the stalk object category so that they are included here with the human forms.

HEAD (pl. 25b) 1 example

There is only one head, a simple one that is conical with the suggestion of a coiled headdress that has broken off (pl. 25b). There were several heads of this kind in the Jarmo collection (Broman Morales 1983, fig.163:7, 8, 10). This head easily could have belonged to any of the three female forms at Çayönü. The piece is oval in section and was broken off its stalk body.

DISCUSSION

The human figurine fragments found in early settlements seem to indicate that the modelers had a need to express a short term wish or desire. If a more permanent object had been required, they had the skill for making very fine objects of stone. Since only one small stone figurine has been found at Çayönü (pl. 25a) and there are none in the collections of Jarmo and Sarab, it seems likely that these clay figures were of momentary importance in the lives of their makers. I reason therefore that clay figurines were made by individuals who were thus expressing their needs or desires. The moment of forming the plastic clay was the moment in which the wish was expressed. The lack of realism in the figure was not important; the identification of the maker was imprinted in the plastic clay at the time of manufacture.

It would seem that each person had free expression as regards the form of the figurine; there is a wide range of forms between the realistic and the abstract and as wide a range of skill in modeling. It was therefore not simply a matter of producing fertility figures. And indeed no demonstrably pregnant examples are to be seen in any of the types described here. Once the wish or desire had been expressed in a modeled object, it could be discarded casually, as is attested by the distribution and fragmentary condition of these small creations. There was nothing formal about either the process or the product.

ABSTRACT FORMS

STALK OBJECTS (pl. 25c-e, g-i) 23 examples

Twenty-three pieces are classified here. A stalk object is basically a cylindrical rod that tapers in varying degrees to a round, flat, or concave base. These pieces therefore stand well. There is only one whole piece (pl. 25c); the top is modified by overlapping pellets pressed over the top. The base is irregularly concave and is indented in such a way as to leave fingernail incisions deeply imbedded in it.

Next is a small, nicely modeled example with a more or less round base that is slightly concave (pl. 25d). There are three small depressions at the edge of the base, as though the figure had been set down on tiny pebbles when left to dry. Finger pressure on the plastic clay formed a flap on one side of the stalk, but this seems to have been unintentional. The piece is slightly tilted and waisted before the stalk is broken off.

Another figurine with a round concave base has an appliquéd pellet on one side just above the base and a depression opposite where another pellet was applied. The waisted stalk rises to a gently rounded "nose." At the back of the stalk, behind the nose, there are two more round pellets, one on each side (pl. 25e). A similar example is very waisted, giving an hour-glass profile, with the enlarged stalk top broken off. A tiny whole example with a round flat base has the top flaring out but broken off. This may represent the torso form.

Eight fragments are tall slender stalks on bases not much greater in diameter than the body (e.g., pl. 25g, i). These resemble the "nails" described in the Jarmo report as stalk objects (Broman Morales 1983, p. 387). The tops are broken off all but one piece which is very hard with a pitted surface. The stalk is oval in section and the top seems to end in a small appliquéd flap. The bottom is flat, so this piece stands well (pl. 25i). A larger piece that resembles the nails but whose sides bulge slightly is almost whole except for its missing top (pl. 25h). The base is flat with rounded edges. This piece rather resembles a small pestle.

Two tall cylindrical stalk sections, one with appliquéd pieces broken off, are included in this group although both bases and tops are missing. There are two tiny pieces of stalk tops included here, one that is slightly pinched at the top with a groove running across the rounded end, and one whose stalk tapers to a flattened top.

There are five bases. Two of them are small with round, flattened bottoms with tapered, slightly waisted stalks that are broken off. Another tiny one has a round concave base. The top has been squashed down while plastic and pellets seem to have been appliquéd on the stalk above the base. A stalk fragment with an oval section has a partially flaked off base which probably was flat. The last one is squat and lumpy with a flat bottom.

ROD SECTIONS 18 examples

There are eighteen rod sections or cylindrical fragments. Both ends are broken off fifteen of these; an end of one is flattened and an end of another comes to a point. The ends of a third are flattened or broken off; the surfaces of the ends are worn. Diameters vary from 6 mm to 12 mm with five examples having diameters of around 8 mm. These pieces are all fragmentary; some may belong to stalk objects.

No interpretation is possible as yet for these stalk objects and related rod sections. In the Jarmo collection 181 examples are placed in this category which so far has still not been well defined. It is assumed that these are abstract forms and probably are related to the human forms. The same is true of the double-winged-base objects.

DOUBLE-WINGED-BASE OBJECT (pl. 25f) 1 example

The only example of this form as yet recovered at Çayönü is a tiny fragment with a worn surface (pl. 25f). One end of the flat base is broken off. The top is a low rounded lump at the base of which there may have been an appliquéd strip. At Jarmo 300 pieces were identified as belonging to this category, while at Sarab the collection was much smaller with only sixty-nine examples in this category. Sarab is considered to date somewhat later than Jarmo and at Jarmo this form so far has been found only in the upper levels. So perhaps the concept portrayed by this shape came too late to have become part of the Çayönü inventory.

STUDS (pl. 25m, n) 2 examples

One whole object and one fragment have been placed here. Both are small, well modeled of fine-grained clay, and very smooth and hard. The whole example is hour-glass shaped (pl. 25n), with round, concave ends, one slightly larger than the other. Presumably the larger end is the base. The other piece is a stalk sheared vertically more or less through the center; one end is broken off while the other is beveled (pl. 25m).

CONES (pl. 25j) 7 examples

There are seven cones, all of them small with basal diameters of 12-15.5 mm (e.g., pl. 25j). Six are more or less whole with only the tips broken off three of them. One with a basal diameter of 9 mm is a fragment with the top and part of the side broken off. The sides of all of the cones slope straight up from the flat round bases. All examples are well made and quite hard. There is no modification either in shape or in surface treatment. Since there are so few examples, they are considered as related to the stalk objects rather than to the geometric forms.

NON-CLASSIFIABLE FRAGMENTS

SPECIAL SHAPED PIECES (pls. 25k, l; 26a-d; and 27i) 23 examples

Twenty-three objects are listed here. Three are whole in the shape of a rod that is "footed" on both ends (pl. 26a-c); one also has a groove on one side. These may have been toggles although they are not perforated. Four other pieces are also rods that have a more or less triangular section. One of these has a reed mat impression on the flat basal surface and what appears to be the same mat impressed on the rounded apex of the triangle (pl. 27i). This piece is carefully shaped of fine-grained clay and there are clear finger facets impressed along one side. Both ends are broken off.

A disc that is missing a piece on the side has been only partially perforated on top (pl. 26d). The base is flat and a piece of clay has been pressed onto the center of that surface to reinforce the perforation that is built up on the other side. The rim of the upper surface is very smooth and rounded. There is a depression around the raised center or "hub." The piece looks very much like the wheel of a toy cart. A fragment of a similar disc resembles this piece in shape and diameter (25 mm).

An oddly shaped, more or less cylindrical object has a rounded base. The ends are rounded to a low pinched ridge on top; this upper surface is flat between the ridges (pl. 25l). Another cylindrical piece has a shelf pinched out across the center (pl. 25k). Both ends are round and slightly concave; the edge of the shelf is rounded. One end is partly broken, but the object stands well on the other end. All of the other fragments have no distinguishing characteristics and cannot be classified.

The section on figurines ends here. It is easy to see that the animal figures and the human forms, although mainly abstract, had a special reason for their creation even if it now eludes us. The abstract forms are more difficult to understand, but the variety of shapes seems to indicate that some thought was behind their manufacture. It is unfortunate that the number of figurines so far recovered at Çayönü is so small, but even 200 or 300 additional pieces would probably not change the picture very much. The largest of the categories is that of the geometric forms (125 examples), which I do not consider to be figurines but counters of some sort, or gaming pieces. Their purpose is fairly clear. In the case of beads, miniature vessels, and other miscellaneous forms, the possible use or the copying of utilitarian objects puts these items into a category apart from that of the figurines.

GEOMETRIC FORMS

BALL-SHAPED OBJECTS (pl. 26e) 43 examples

There are forty-three balls, four of which have one slightly flattened surface (e.g., pl. 26e). Two are flattened ovoids and five are fragments. The range in size is from 25-30 mm in diameter (four of these) to 7-10 mm in diameter (three of these). The majority are in the 15-25 mm range. The balls are smooth surfaced and hard. Some are slightly faceted by finger pressure during manufacture and a few were fashioned by rolling the plastic clay between the palms.

Balls have been found wherever clay figurines appear. It may be assumed that clay balls were used as counters, but they may have served as marbles or sling missiles.

DISC-SHAPED OBJECTS (pl. 26f-k) 35 examples

These discs, of which there are thirty-five, show considerable difference in form and size. Four are plano-concave in section and resemble shallow little dishes with rounded edges (e.g., pl. 26f, g). Eight are bi-convex; six of these are small, lentoid in shape, smooth surfaced, and have diameters between 9 and 19 mm (e.g., pl. 26h). Another with a diameter of 23 mm is well made and burned black. The last bi-convex example has deep flat reed impressions on one surface and line incisions on the other.

Six discs are plano-convex; one of these is rather roughly shaped and two others are marked on both faces by linear markings of flat reeds onto which the plastic clay was pressed (pl. 26i-k). The disc illustrated on plate 26i has had most of one surface flaked off in antiquity, but the remaining portion shows the linear marks. One tiny piece (diameter 10-11 mm) looks like a gumdrop. A larger disc with a diameter of 29.5 mm is thin and well made; it is smooth on both surfaces. The last plano-convex piece is faceted on top and shows a palm print on the flattened surface.

Nine discs are bi-plano; these are thick with rounded edges. Sizes range from 10 to 26 mm in diameter. There are three examples of concavo-convex discs. On one of these the convex surface shows a palm print on a smooth part. This piece is more or less round with a pitted surface and a diameter of 39-42 mm. Another disc is hard and black with a flat beveled edge, part of which is broken off. This piece is nicely rounded with a very shallow concavity. The last example is small with a diameter of 17 mm; it is very slightly concavo-convex. The concavity is lightly striated while the convex surface is smooth. Two small discs with diameters of 20 mm are slightly concave on both surfaces. The two discs are whole and well made with smooth depressions on one side and slight faceting on the other.

All of these discs are more or less round and well shaped; like the balls, they could represent counters.

PERFORATED DISCS AND PERFORATED OBJECTS 10 examples

There are ten pieces in this division; three are disc fragments with estimated diameters of the perforations ranging from 8 to 12 mm and exterior diameters of 52 mm. Two of these are bi-convex in section and one is concavo-convex. Another piece is a fragment of a flattened oval with an estimated diameter of 6 mm for the perforation. There is a very irregular fragment that is quite thick in section; the diameter of the perforation is 3 mm.

The other five objects are shaped like spindle whorls but could not have been used as such because the holes are too small. Three are whole and two are fragments. The three whole examples are bi-convex; one is not collared around the perforation, one is slightly collared, and the last one has pronounced lipped edges around the perforation.

RING DISCS (pl. 26l) 3 examples

There are three fragments of flat ring discs (e.g., pl. 26l). This shape also appears in the ground stone category where all of the examples are fragments of a quarter of a circle or less. The best modeled clay fragment has nicely rounded exterior edges and straight interior edges. The exterior diameter is estimated to be 60 mm, while the diameter of the perforation is 25 mm.

The other two discs have thinner sections, again with rounded external edges, and external diameters estimated at 31 and 36 mm. The interior diameters are 19 and 21 mm. It is difficult to say how or for what purpose these objects were used.

PELLET-SHAPED OBJECT (pl. 27g) 22 examples

Eight objects are classified here, but three of them are fragments. They simply may be formings of plastic clay not related to the manufacture of figurines. In addition, fourteen pieces are classified as flattened pellets; five are whole and nine are fragments. These are generally small with bi-plano or plano-convex sections. All are hard and made of fine-grained clay, well modeled, and smooth surfaced. One tiny example is surely a breast measuring 10 mm by 7 mm. Another has one surface covered with tiny punctates (pl. 27g). The base is very smooth and flat. A piece of bone of comparable size has had multiple tiny holes drilled into it (Çambel and Braidwood 1980, pl. 46:21). These flattened pellets may have been counters of some sort. At least they would seem to have been more specialized than the five amorphous pellets.

MISCELLANEOUS FORMS

BEADS (pl. 27d-f) 11 examples

There are only eleven clay beads, six whole and five fragments. At the same time there is a large collection of stone beads and bead blanks. In stone, the most common form is the short cylinder bead for which the bead blanks were prepared. Pebbles were also used to form pendants and other forms of beads. It would seem, therefore, that clay was not considered an adequate material for bead manufacture. In fact, one of the clay beads was squashed flat at one end while still plastic (pl. 27f). Another one is a short cylinder bead, not very well made, with the perforation quite off center (pl. 27e). This bead probably was formed over a straw that burned out in the firing. The next example is a flattened barrel bead broken at each end (pl. 27d). Striations visible on the sides of the perforation indicate that this bead was also formed over a straw or tiny stick. Another whole bead is similar in size and shape. There is a tiny whole bead that is short and bi-convex; the diameter is 8 mm and the length of the off-center perforation is 5.5 mm. The last whole example is roughly rounded with a very narrow perforation.

Of the fragments, three are flattened barrel beads and two are cylinder beads, one round in section with a flat end and the other flattened with an oval section.

MINIATURE VESSEL FRAGMENTS (pl. 27h) 3 examples

There are three fragments which suggest small bowls. They all have simple silhouettes; the wall rises from a thick rounded base to a thinner finished rim. The more complete example shows a smoothed but lumpy exterior, while the interior is more carefully smoothed (pl. 27h). The diameter of the rim is estimated to be 35 mm while the greatest wall thickness at the base is 4.5 mm. The second example is about the same size but is crudely shaped with a more shallow concavity. The third bowl fragment has a much thicker base and not enough of the rim remains to determine the diameter. There is also a fragment that appears to be the base of a stemmed vessel; the base is round and slightly concave and the interior is smooth and rounded at the bottom. The material used in the manufacture of this piece is quite soft and the surfaces are very eroded.

STAMP SEALS (pl. 27a, b) 2 examples

The larger of the two stamps is a wedge-shaped piece with a cavity in the upper end which shows that it was perhaps hafted; a pair of joined arches in the shape of a script letter "m" are modeled at the lower end (pl. 27a). The stamp end is flat and has a granular surface. It appears that this end was modeled first and then clay was added to form the crudely shaped body. This part is lumpy, rough surfaced, and includes several small pebbles. One surface of the piece is flatter than the other. Some flat pellets are pressed onto this surface with several clustered toward the tapered end. This end is broken off but there remains in it a cavity of 8 mm diameter and 35 mm depth; striations on the walls of this cavity show that the body of the stamp was molded over a stick. Although the stamp is of clay, it is brick-hard and could have been pressed into plastic clay or it could have been used to print fabrics or hides. There is, however, no trace of color or any other substance left on the stamp.

The other, smaller, stamp is also broken at the upper end (pl. 27b). In size and shape it closely resembles the stamp seal reported at Jarmo (Broman Morales 1983, p. 389 and fig. 170:1). The Jarmo stamp has a rather crude spiral deeply incised on the flat base. The stamp at Çayönü is more carefully prepared and consists of three concentric circles. The central hole is deeper than the circles and is perfectly round. The edges of the outer circle seem to be battered and worn. A "cuff" of clay around the stamp end may have served as reinforcement. As is the case with the larger stamp above, there are no traces of color.

SMOOTHER (pl. 27c) 1 example

A round knob-shaped object with a flat, very smooth base is difficult to interpret (pl. 27c). The top is a flattened oval in shape and is cracked where it joins the base, which indicates the mode of manufacture. The base is also oval in shape with an old worn break on one end and a fresh break on the other. This object is carefully made.

HOUSE MODELS (pl. 30a, b) 5 examples

Two of these extraordinary objects were found in the burned house, U 9, which is a cell building. From field photographs it has been possible to reconstruct the dimensions of the larger model (U 9-2/8). The smaller model (U 9-2/14) has been reconstructed, although some fragments are missing (pl. 30a, b).

Essentially these models are clay boxes that have thick chaff-tempered walls which are roughly smoothed, a high floor (about 40 mm from floor to base) which leaves room for cells underneath, a rectangular doorway, and a roof of clay that is plastered over sticks which are laid across the walls from one side to the other. A low parapet, about 20 mm high, encircles the roof and has a U-shaped drain in its center over the back wall. The sticks resting on the base to support the floor are laid the length of the walls, while the sticks that support the roof are laid from side to side.

A perforation under the floor on the left of the doorway of the larger model is 5 mm in diameter and may represent a vent hole that would help to confirm the cell plan underlying the house.

By comparing the measurements of these two models, it becomes apparent that very similar proportions were used in both, but one model is larger than the other. The small example measures 115 mm (end walls) by 130 mm (side walls), while the larger measures 150 mm by 180 mm. The walls are 20-30 mm thick.

Two additional pieces of roof parapet fit together to form the front section (corner to corner on the inside surface) of a fragment that may represent a third house model (19M 2-23/16-19). The impression of a stick support is under the length of the fragment. The outer length of this piece is about 115 mm and compares well with the smaller model (U 9-2/14). The height of these parapet fragments is about 36 mm, while the U 9-2/14 parapet height is only 20 mm.

Fragments of a fourth house model (25K 4-12/2) were found in 1984 during the removal of a balk. The house model pieces were mingled with tumbled mud brick and were very dry and fragile. It could be established that these fragments represent a back wall, with parapet and U-shaped drain, the complete wall of the right side from the back corner to the front where there is an edge of the doorway, and the left side wall with an edge of the doorway in front. A detailed description follows since this model is too heavy and too friable ever to be reconstructed.

The walls are 40 mm thick and the back wall measures 180 mm across at roof level. The height of the doorway is estimated to be 60 mm. As yet there are no clear joins for the walls, but they must belong to the same model since wall thickness is the same for all of the pieces. There are stick impressions over the top of the right wall.

These walls were shaped as flattened rectangles with the ends rounded; they were then set up on sticks which supported the floor and the corners were thickly plastered to seal the joins. This clay box was plastered again on the outside with a layer of tempered mud about 5 mm thick. This mode of manufacture accounts for the very heavy walls which in turn caused the easy disintegration of this model.

There is also a corner fragment of a roof parapet. Only this one piece has been recovered from this particular model, but it indicates a much smaller house. From the outside corner to the edge of the U-shaped drain the measurement is 30 mm. For the U 9-2/14 model the same measurement is 55 mm. The parapet wall thickness for the fragment is 9 mm, while that of the U 9 model is 12 mm.

The fact that all of these models were complete, with roof and roof parapet, suggests that they were only made to represent houses. It does not seem likely that these models were either wish figures or working models for builders. For the moment there is no explanation as to their purpose. All of these models are associated with cell buildings.

PESTLE-SHAPED OBJECTS (pl. 28) 6 examples

Six objects are classified as pestle-shaped. It is not certain that any of them were ever actually used for pounding or grinding; it is their shape that suggests the term "pestle-shaped form." The largest, most complete, and best modeled of these examples is conical with a saddle-shaped concavity for the base and a deep round-bottomed cavity in the top (pl. 28). This object is heavy and brick-like; a certain amount of concretion has adhered to one side and part of the concavity of the base. There is a pebble inclusion on the inside wall of the top cavity and parts of the rim have broken off. Since the bottom of the cavity is wide as well as smooth and rounded, this hole could not have been intended for hafting. The piece stands well although it tilts to one side. Its use or purpose is not possible to determine.

Another piece, shaped somewhat like the first except that the top is smooth and rounded, is also heavy and brick-like. The basal edge is battered, with old and worn breaks, and the sloping base is smooth and slightly saddled. A comparable form, pear-shaped rather than conical, tapers to a rounded top and has a flat base. This object is very hard and is covered with concretions. The piece is heavy and fits the hand nicely; the base seems to have been use-flattened.

Two other pieces are about the same size with a height of 50 mm and a diameter of 40 mm. The sides are straight and both ends are flattened. One example, which came from the burned house, U 9, is very smooth and blackened. There are facets, probably worn breaks, around the edge of the base. These are smoothed, but it cannot be determined by what use. The other piece has a very rough surface with impressions of grass or straw and other inclusions. There is no sign of use or wear which would be hard to detect in any case on this rough surface.

Finally there is one small piece; it is hard and brick-like with a slightly convex base. It tapers slightly to a break which shows that it was molded around a flat stick. This suggests that this piece was hafted. The height of this object is 32 mm and the diameter of the base is about 18 mm.

SHALLOW BASINS (pl. 29a-d) 6 examples

Six basins are described here. Two small round basins were found whole (pl. 29a, b). They are made of chaff or fiber tempered clay and are well fired. The bases are flat but roughly surfaced, while the interiors and low rounded rims are carefully modeled and smoothed. These basins could have served as measures for something dry, such as salt or seeds. The diameters are 130-133 mm and 156 mm.

A larger basin which is in two fragments resembles the small basins. It is white, made of chaff or fiber tempered clay, and has a roughly surfaced flat bottom. The interior is smoothed; the low rim has disintegrated. The diameter is about 223 mm (Çambel and Braidwood 1980, pl. 47:10).

The fourth example seems to have been formed by pressing wet clay mixed with chaff down into the bottom of a reed basket. The interior of this clay surface was then smoothed and brought up to form a low rim (Çambel and Braidwood 1980, pl. 47:9). A good impression of the bottom and lower two or three coils of the basket results from this procedure (cf. Broman Morales 1983, fig. 169:14 and appended comment by J. M. Adovasio, p. 425). It seems unlikely that such a thick clay base (55 mm) was put in to make the basket impermeable. The clay may have been mixed in the basket for use as a plaster; the remaining material could have hardened and been discarded. This piece was found in the U 9 house and was burned when the house caught fire.

A roughly rectangular basin with rounded corners was found in the corner of a cell of a house; it had fallen into the cell from the room above. It measures 200 mm long and has a thick base. The walls of this basin are low and the rim is rounded (pl. 29c).

The last piece is not really a basin; it is U-shaped in plan with no wall at the open end of the U (pl. 29d). The base is quite thick, measuring 145 mm, and the wall is 27 mm thick. The interior is only 35 mm deep. A spout which forms a lip out over the exterior edge is at the bottom of the U at one end. This has been made by pushing out the plastic clay of the wall during manufacture. This piece was found on the pebble floor of a cell. It is not possible to even guess at the use or purpose of this strange object.

CONCLUSIONS

Figurines and other objects of clay added to the Çayönü inventory (first made in 1984) raised the count from 200 to 400 examples. The newly recorded material from the end of the 1984 season, plus that of the 1985, 1986, and 1987 seasons, fit into the established categories with no difficulty. It is to be assumed, therefore, that any additional shaped clay material would not change the basic inventory.

The small number of examples makes it impossible to get an adequate picture of distribution through time and space. It does seem clear, however, that clay figurines and geometric forms were found exclusively in the domestic occupation areas. No pieces have been inventoried from any of the special buildings.

That there was some sort of ceremonial activity now seems abundantly clear, but the clay figurines were not ceremonial figures nor were they found in concentrations. These circumstances indicate to me the purely personal short term use of the figurines.

CATALOG 2

Illustrated Figurines and Clay Objects from Cayönü

Plate	*Classification*	*Findspot*	*Year*	*Catalog No.*
19a	Animal Figurine: Horned	SA 7-3/2	1972	F.32
19b	Animal Figurine: Horned	21M 3-4/7	1981	F.9
19c	Animal Figurine: Horned	21M 4-0/1	1981	F.3
19d	Animal Figurine: Horned	25K 1-3/2	1987	F.8
19e	Animal Figurine: Horned	R 17-1/1	1970	F.11
19f	Animal Figurine: Horned	25L 2-6/2	1987	F.9
20a	Animal Figurine: Horned(?)	LB 4/5	1968	F.17
20b	Animal Figurine: Horned(?)	R1	1970	F.56
20c	Animal Figurine: Horned(?)	21M cl/3	1984	F.10
20d	Animal Figurine: Horned	SE 5-0/2	1972	F.7
20e	Animal Figurine: Horn Fragment	U 4-8/1	1970	F.36
20f	Animal Figurine: Horned	U 4-0/1	1970	F.37
20g	Animal Figurine: Curly-Tailed Dog	SA 1-3	1968	F.29
20h	Animal Figurine: Curly-Tailed Dog	25L 3-36/5	1987	F.36
20i	Animal Figurine: Curly-Tailed Dog	S 1-10/1	1972	F.33
21a	Animal Figurine: Wild Pig	P 7-16/1	1970	F.12
21b	Animal Figurine: Wild Pig	U 17-2/1	1972	F.6
21c	Animal Figurine: Non-Classifiable Fragment	T 2-3/1	1970	F.21
21d	Animal Figurine: Non-Classifiable Fragment	SE1-0/1	1972	F.2
21e	Animal Figurine: Non-Classifiable Fragment	LB 4/3	1968	F.8
21f	Animal Figurine: Non-Classifiable Fragment	U 5-5/1	1970	F.13
22a	Human Figurine: Simple Seated Form	K6 4	1964	F.10
22b	Human Figurine: Abstract Form, "Lady Stalk"	U 5-0/1	1970	F.3
22c	Human Figurine: Simple Seated Form	K5 sf-1	1964	F.11
22d	Human Figurine: Simple Seated Form	20L 2-3/20	1980	F.4
22e	Human Figurine: Simple Seated Form	C 3-6	1970	F.49
22f	Human Figurine: Simple Seated Form	R 20-2	1970	F.53
22g	Human Figurine: Abstract Form, "Lady Stalk"	25K 3-25/8	1987	F.64

Catalog 2. Illustrated Figurines and Clay Objects from Cayönü—cont.

Plate	*Classification*	*Findspot*	*Year*	*Catalog No.*
22h	Human Figurine: Simple Seated Form	K8-9 sf-1	1964	F.8
22i	Human Figurine: Abstract Form, "Lady Stalk"	9. 25K 3-28/1	1987	F.63
23a	Human Figurine: Abstract Form, "Lady Stalk"	1. 26K 1-7/2	1987	F.13
23b	Human Figurine: Abstract Form, "Lady Stalk"	27K 3-10/3	1987	F.76
23c	Human Figurine: Abstract Form, "Lady Stalk"	20M 8-48/188	1987	F.68
23d	Human Figurine: Composite Form, Female	DF 2-6/11	1985	F.12
23e	Human Figurine: Composite Form, Female	SA 8-5/1	1972	F.28
23f	Human Figurine: Composite Form, Female	SAl 2	1968	F.1
23g	Human Figurine: Composite Form, Female	SA 0-3/1	1972	F.12
24a	Human Figurine: Head and Torso Fragment	28-29M cl/13	1980	F.18
24b	Human Figurine: Torso Fragment	AD 0-0/1	1972	F.8
24c	Human Figurine: Torso Fragment	U 3-55	1970	F.15
24d	Human Figurine: Head and Torso Fragment	C 1-0/1	1970	F.14
24e	Human Figurine: Torso Fragment	20M 5-45/31	1984	F.30
24f	Human Figurine: Torso Fragment	U 22-5	1972	F.29
24g	Human Figurine: Head and Torso Fragment	20L 3-0/3	1981	F.10
24h	Human Figurine: Head and Torso Fragment	20N 5-10/1	1984	F.31
24i	Human Figurine: Head and Torso Fragment	28K cl 26/1	1981	F.5
24j	Human Figurine: Torso Fragment	CF 2-20/1	1984	F.15
25a	Abstract Form: Stone Human Figurine	30L cl/8		
25b	Abstract Form: Human Figurine Head Fragment	BN 1	1968	F.19
25c	Abstract Form: "Stalk" Object	LB 4-2	1968	F.4
25d	Abstract Form: "Stalk" Object	X 2-11	1970	F.52
25e	Abstract Form: "Stalk" Object	20M 8-48/10	1986	F.23
25f	Abstract Form: Double-Winged-Base Object	SB1 2	1968	F.14
25g	Abstract Form: "Stalk" Object	28K cl 22/1	1981	F.4
25h	Abstract Form: "Stalk" Object	SA 7-3/1	1972	F.18
25i	Abstract Form: "Stalk" Object	U 3-55	1970	F.2
25j	Abstract Form: Cone	U 17-2/2	1972	F.4
25k	Non-Classifiable Fragment: Cylindrical-Shaped Object	27L 5-7/13	1986	F.37
25l	Non-Classifiable Fragment: Cylindrical-Shaped Object	20M 8-48/100	1987	F.24
25m	Abstract Form: Stud	QC 5 4	1968	F.9
25n	Abstract Form: Stud	K6 5	1964	F.22
26a	Non-Classifiable Fragment: Rod-Shaped and "Footed" Object	AD 2-0/1	1972	F.3
26b	Non-Classifiable Fragment: Rod-Shaped and "Footed" Object	19M 7-33/14	1986	F.28

Catalog 2. Illustrated Figurines and Clay Objects from Cayönü—cont.

Plate	*Classification*	*Findspot*	*Year*	*Catalog No.*
26c	Non-Classifiable Fragment: Rod-Shaped and "Footed" Object	20N 6-25/17	1986	F.11
26d	Non-Classifiable Fragment: Disc-Shaped Object	G 1-0	1970	F.20
26e	Non-Classifiable Fragment: Ball-Shaped Object	G 8-0	1970	F.24
26f	Non-Classifiable Fragment: Disc-Shaped Object	LB 4-2	1968	F.23
26g	Non-Classifiable Fragment: Disc-Shaped Object	20L 4-55/1	1984	F.13
26h	Non-Classifiable Fragment: Disc-Shaped Object	K5-6 sf-1	1964	F.27
26i	Non-Classifiable Fragment: Disc-Shaped Object	K5 4-5	1964	F.28
26j	Non-Classifiable Fragment: Disc-Shaped Object	KW 4-3/3	1978	F.1
26k	Non-Classifiable Fragment: Disc-Shaped Object	20M 3-43/3	1984	F.9
26l	Non-Classifiable Fragment: Flat Ring Disc	Z 4-0/1	1970	F.19
27a	Miscellaneous Form: Stamp Seal	U 9 -0/1	1970	F.46
27b	Miscellaneous Form: Stamp Seal	20M 1-0/8	1980	F.11
27c	Miscellaneous Form: Smoother	20L cl/1	1984	F.1
27d	Miscellaneous Form: Bead	K6 5-6	1964	F.36
27e	Miscellaneous Form: Bead	U 9-0/1	1970	F.18
27f	Miscellaneous Form: Bead	20L 2-cl/87	1980	F.8
27g	Geometric Form: Pellet-Shaped Object	CD 3-31/91	1980	F.9
27h	Miscellaneous Form: Miniature Vessel	K5-6 sf-1	1964	F.5
27i	Non-Classifiable Fragment: Triangular-Shaped Rod	29K 2-5	1981	F.17
28	Miscellaneous Form: Pestle-Shaped Object	AD (RB) 2-32/10	1978	F.3
29a	Miscellaneous Form: Shallow Basin	BNE 3	1968	F.31
29b	Miscellaneous Form: Shallow Basin	S O-1	1970	F.55
29c	Miscellaneous Form: Shallow Basin	20L 2-11/29		
29d	Miscellaneous Form: Shallow "Basin" with One End Open	CE (19M)2-9/47	1980	F.19
30a	House Model	U 9 -2/14	1970	F.5
30b	House Model	U 9 -2/14	1970	F.5

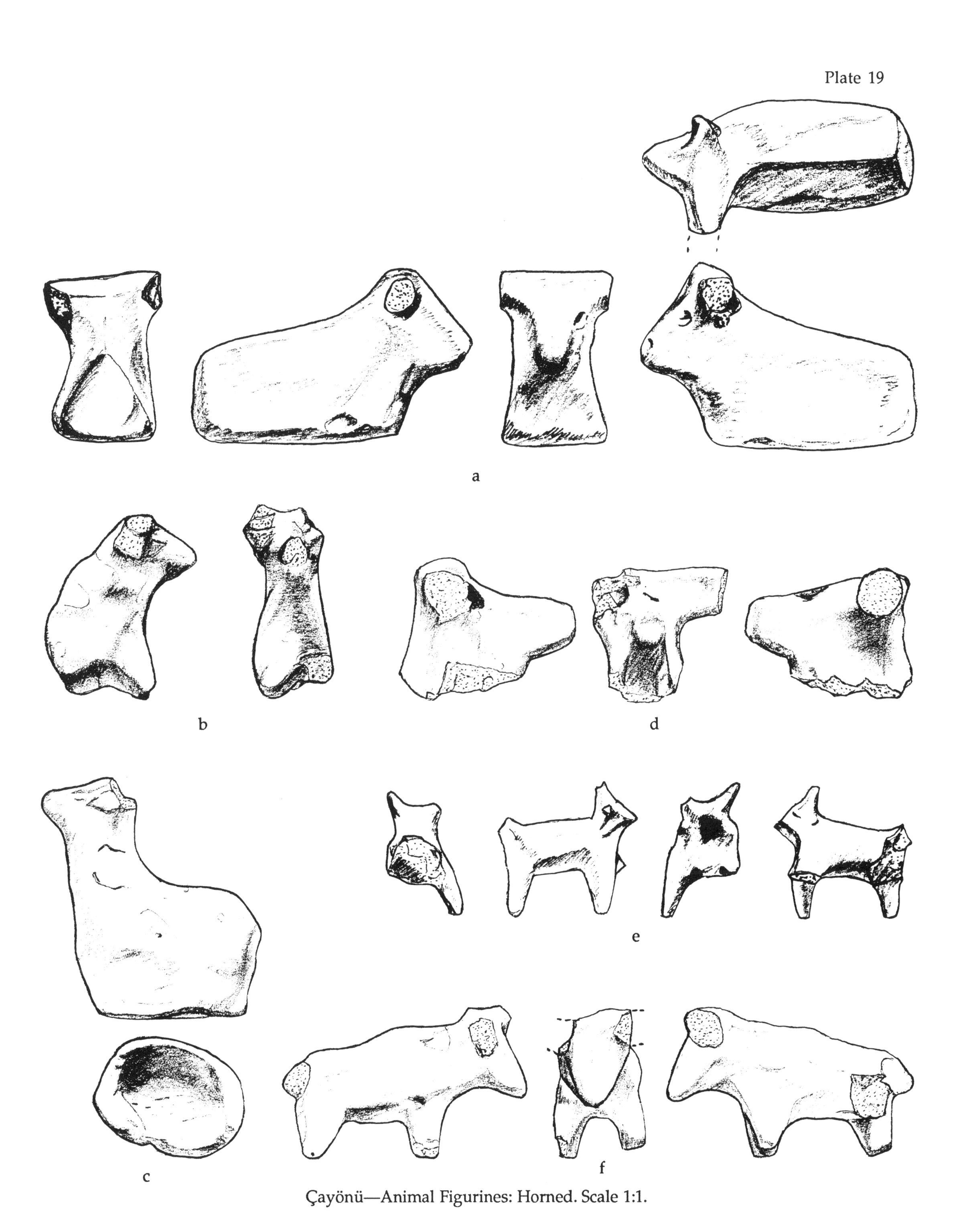

Çayönü—Animal Figurines: Horned. Scale 1:1.

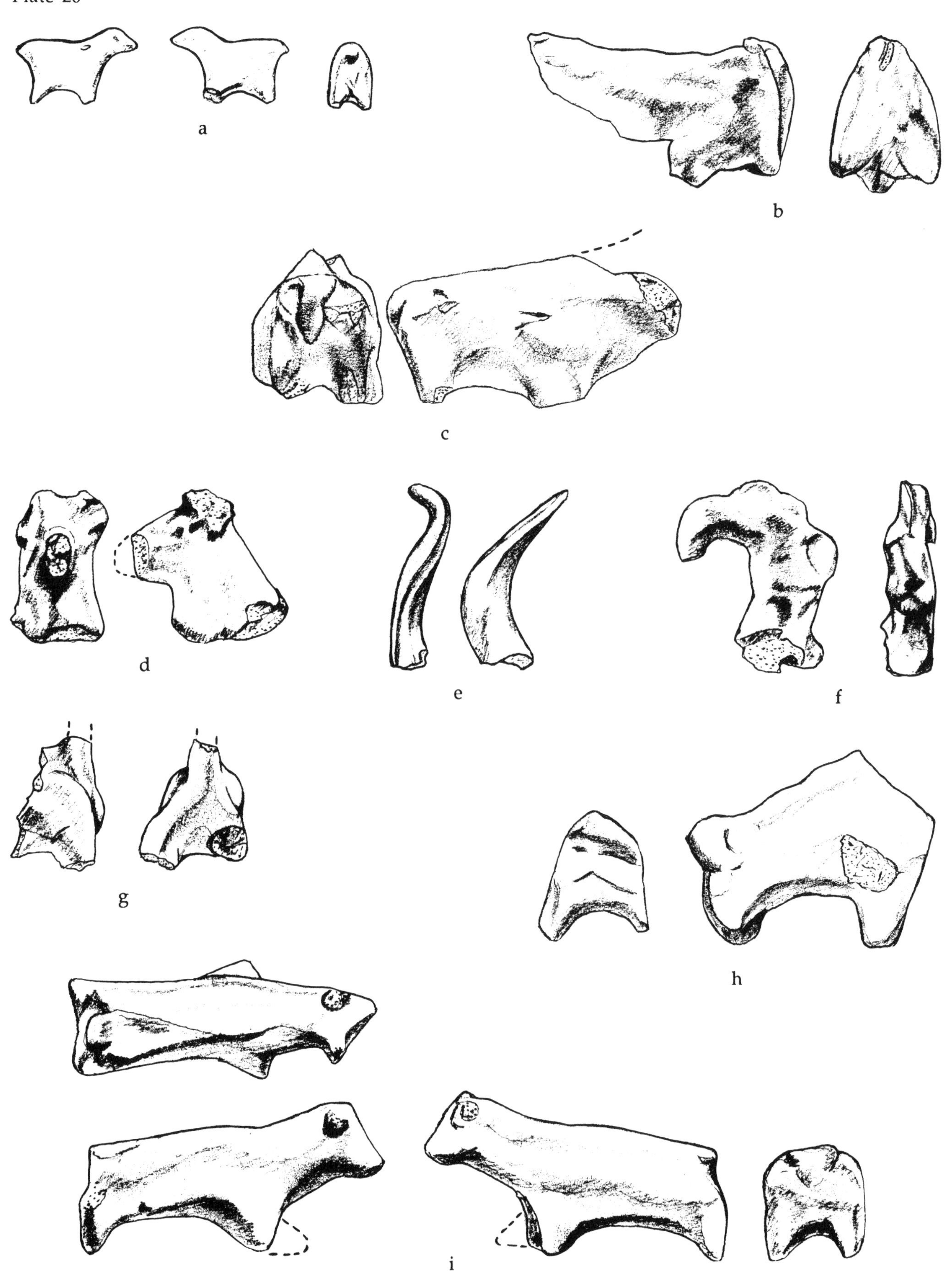

Çayönü—Animal Figurines: (*a-c*) Horned?, (*d, f*) Horned, (*e*) Horn Fragment, and (*g-i*) Curly-Tailed Dogs. Scale 1:1.

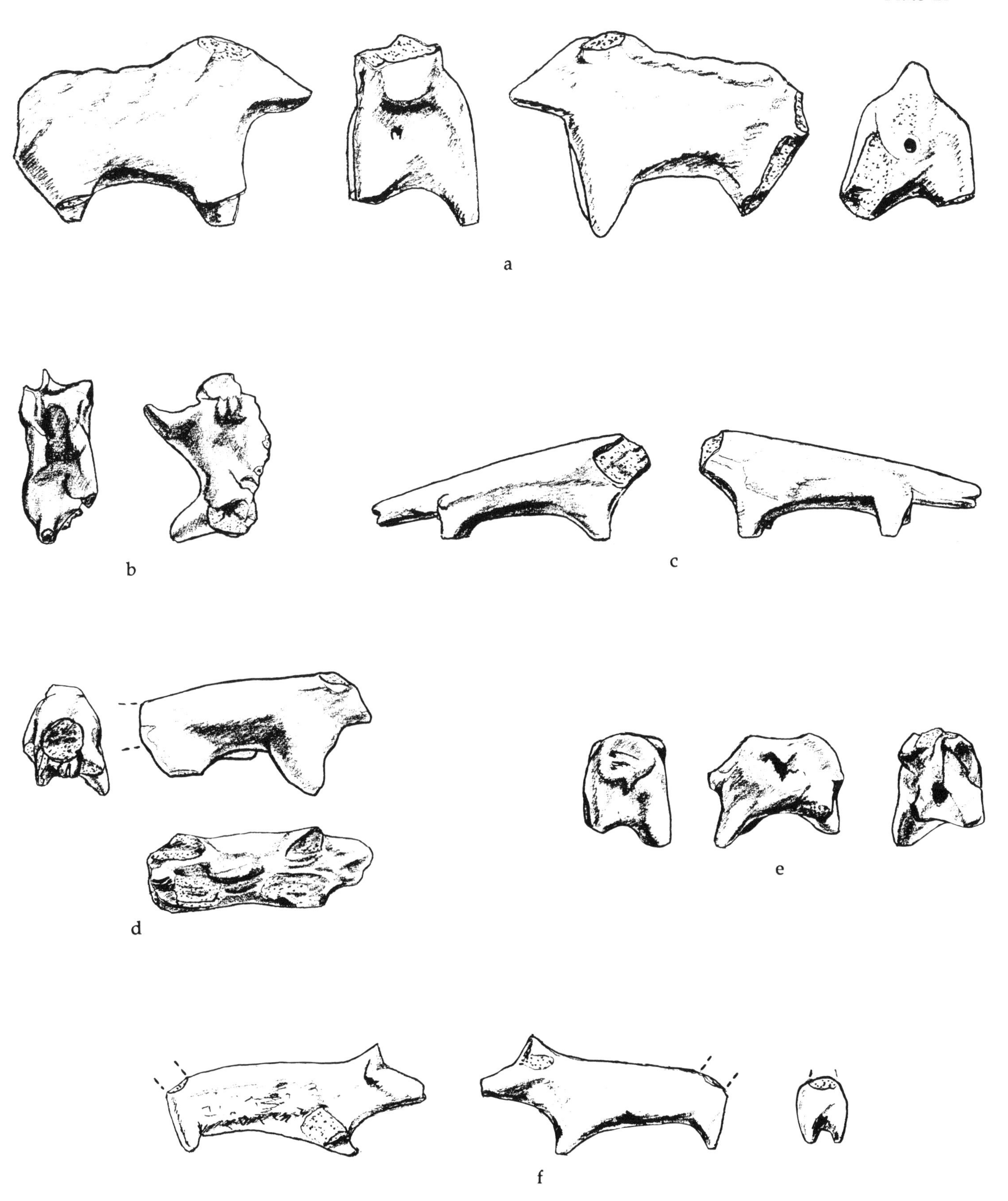

Çayönü—Animal Figurines: (*a, b*) Wild Pigs and (*c-f*) Non-Classifiable Fragments. Scale 1:1.

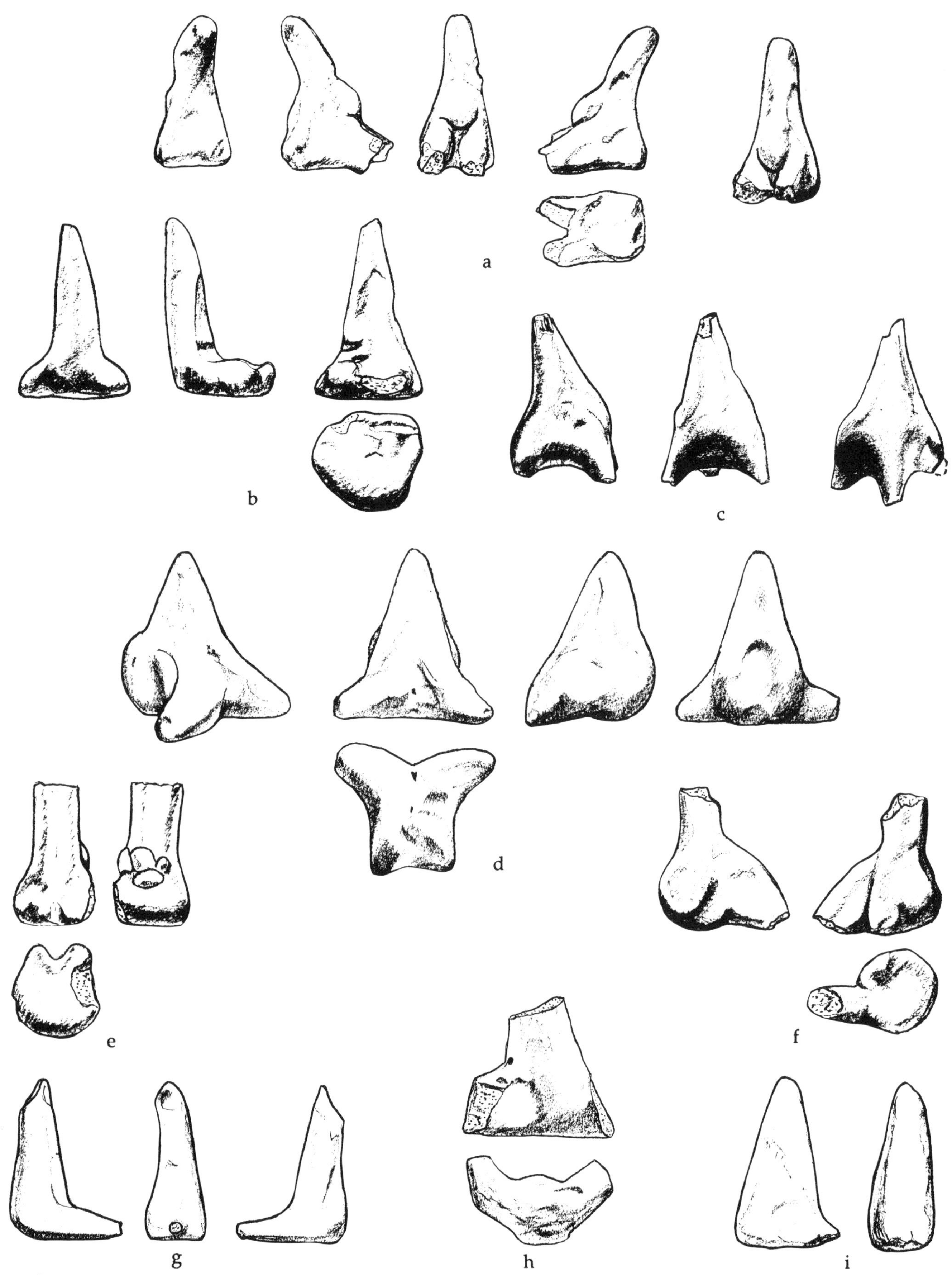

Çayönü—Human Figurines: (*a*, *c-f*, and *h*) Simple Seated Form and (*b*, *g*, *i*) Abstract Form, "Lady Stalks." Scale 1:1.

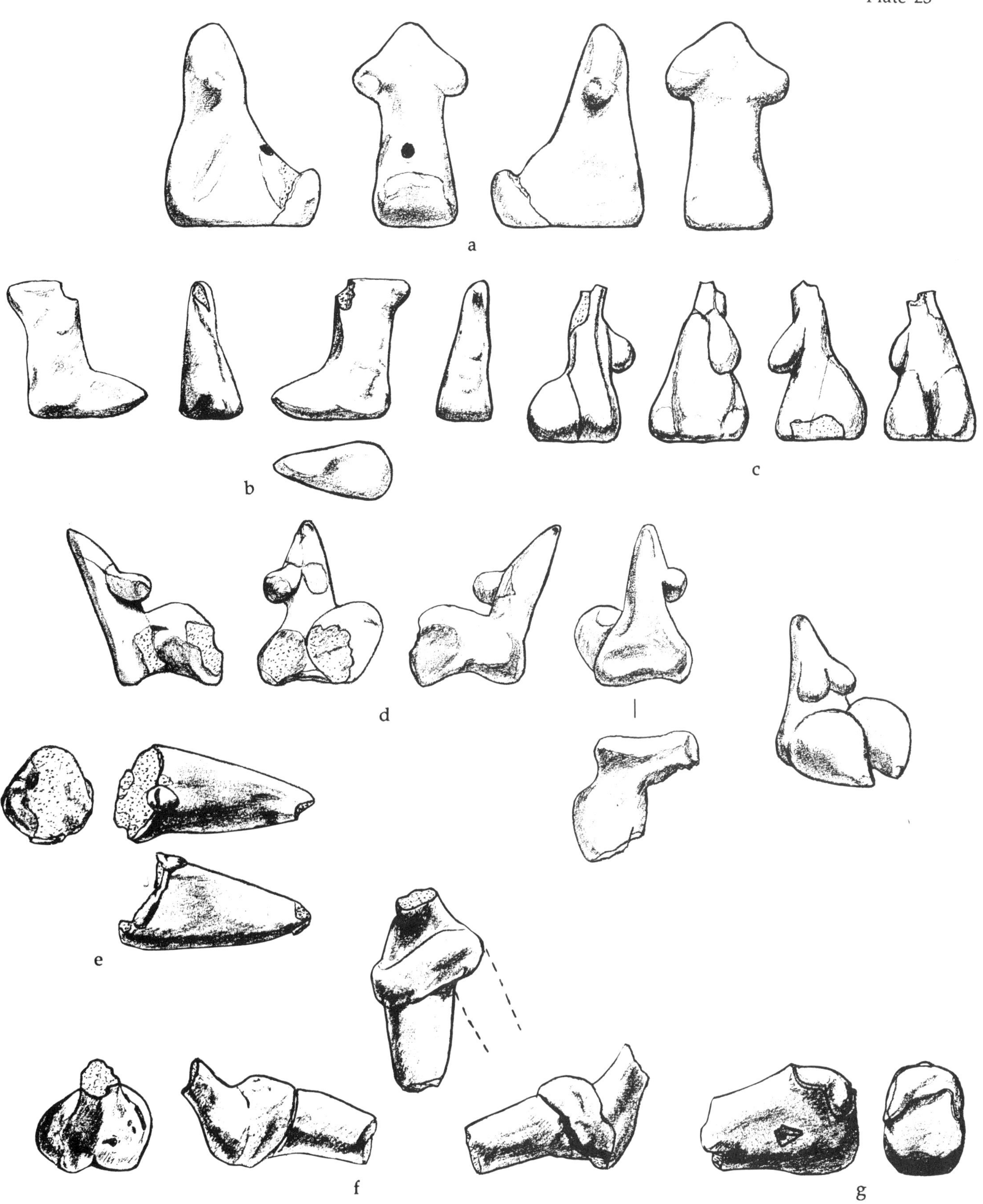

Çayönü—Human Figurines: (*a-c*) Abstract Form, "Lady Stalks" and (*d-g*) Composite Form, Females. Scale 1:1.

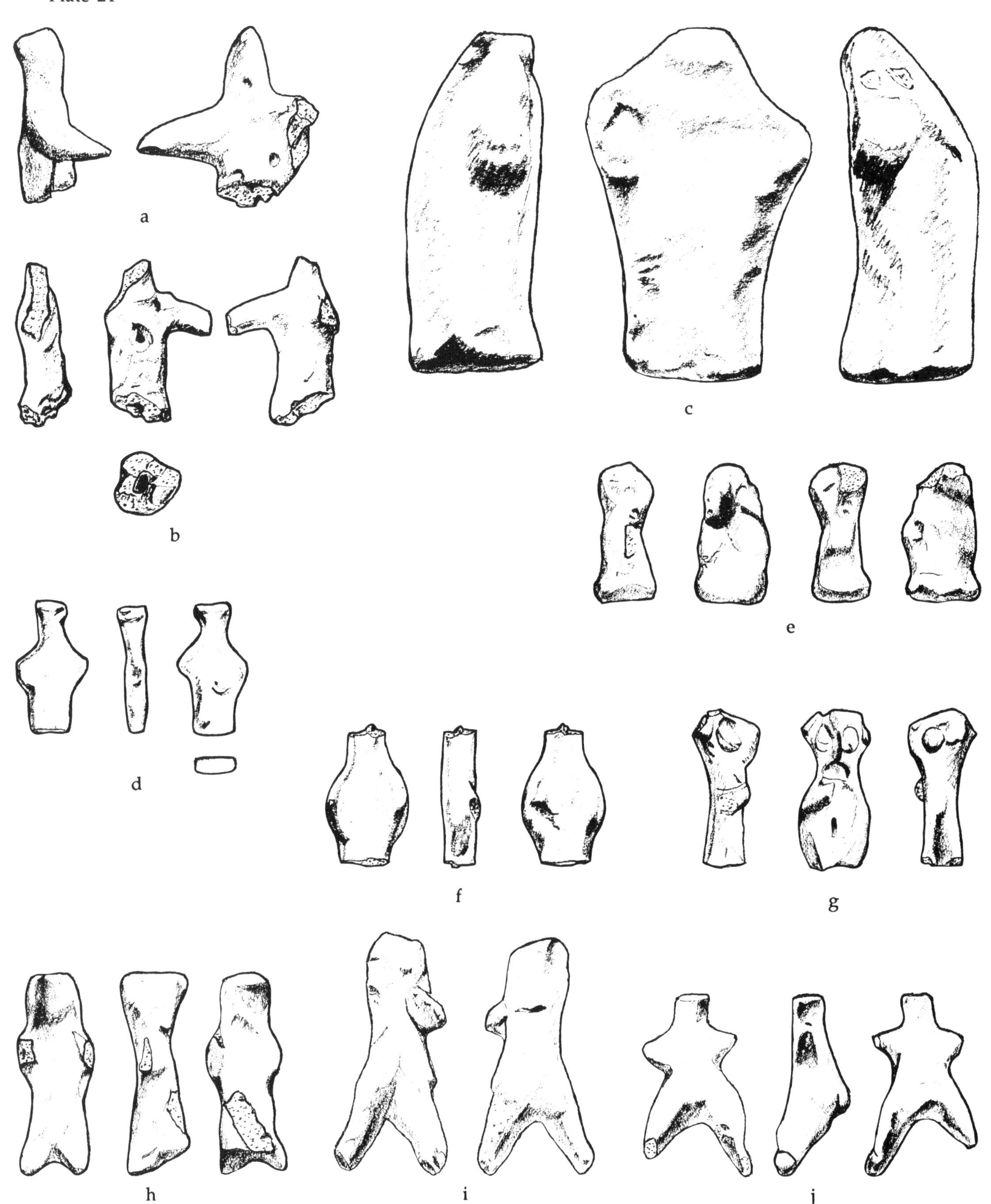

Çayönü—Human Figurines: (*a*, *d*, and *g-i*) Head and Torso Fragments and (*b*, *c*, *e*, *f*, and *j*) Torso Fragments. Scale 1:1.

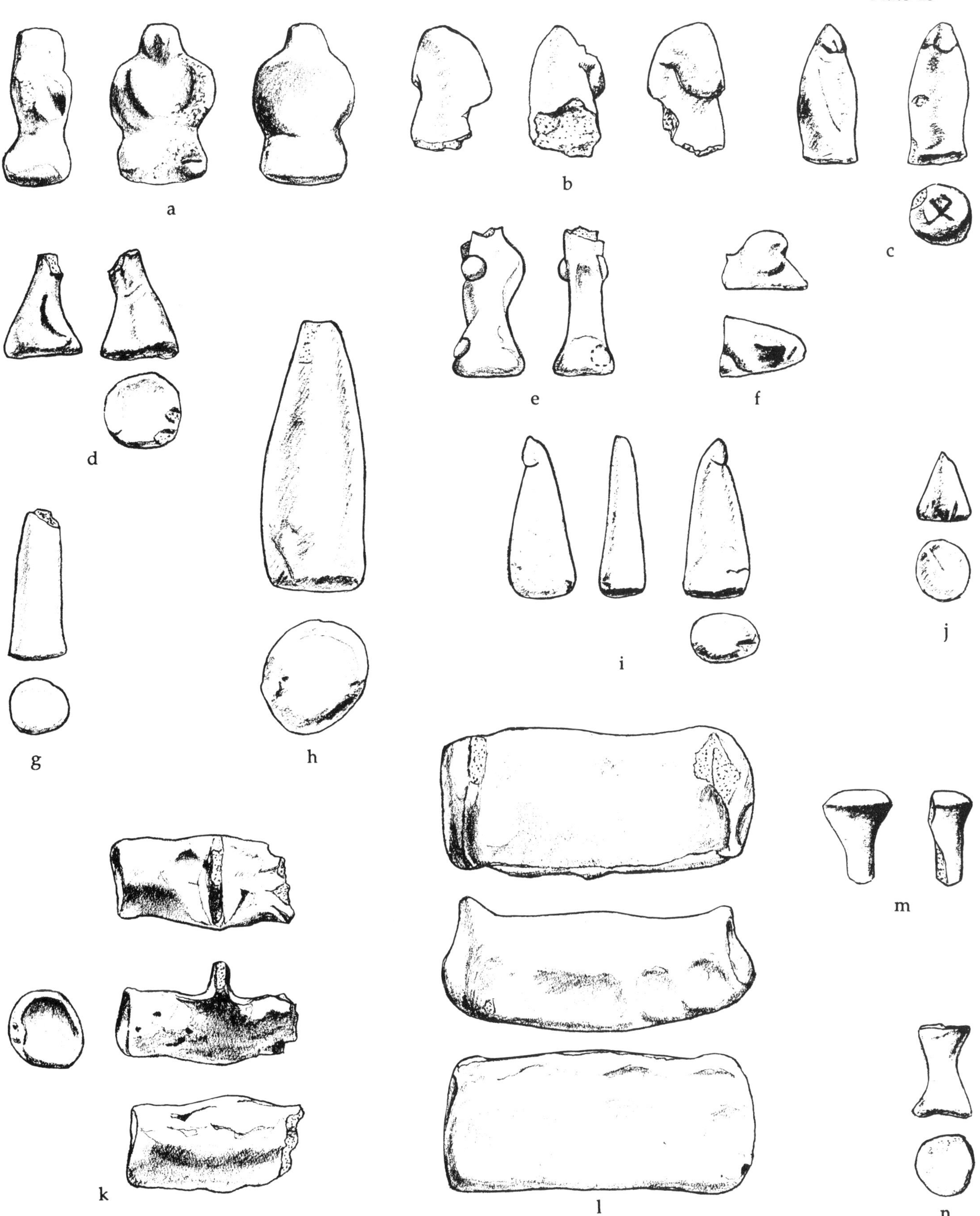

Çayönü—Abstract and Non-Classifiable Fragment Forms: (*a*) Abstract Stone Human Figurine, (*b*) Abstract Human Figurine Head Fragment, (*c-e, g-i*) Abstract "Stalk" Objects, (*f*) Abstract Double-Winged-Base Object, (*j*) Abstract Cone, (*k, l*) Non-Classifiable Cylindrical-Shaped Objects, and (*m, n*) Abstract Studs. Scale 1:1.

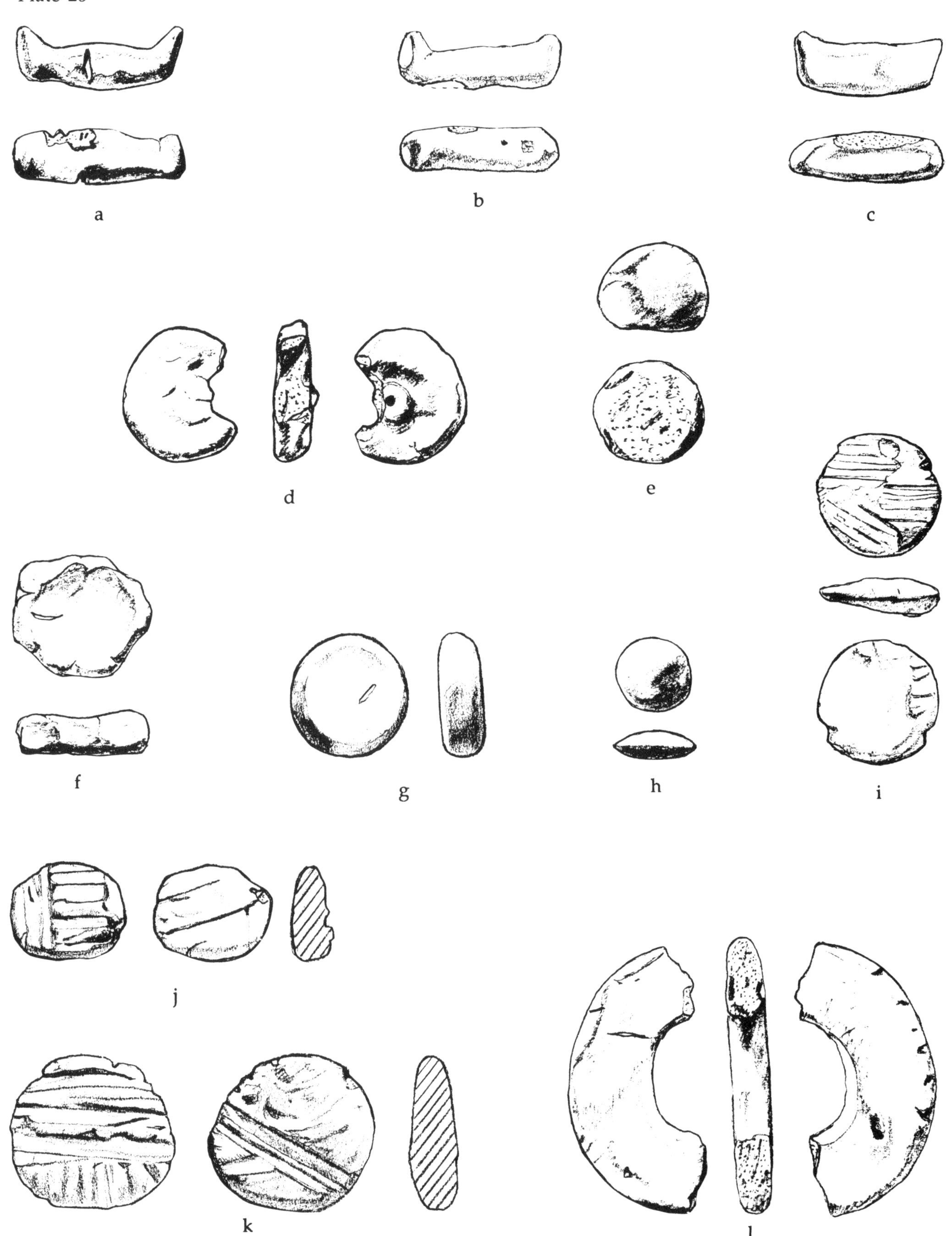

Çayönü—Non-Classifiable Fragments and Geometric Forms: (*a-c*) Non-Classifiable Rod-Shaped and "Footed" Objects, (*d*) Non-Classifiable Disc-Shaped Object, (*e*) Geometric Ball-Shaped Object, (*f-k*) Geometric Disc-Shaped Objects, and (*l*) Geometric Flat Ring Disc. Scale 1:1.

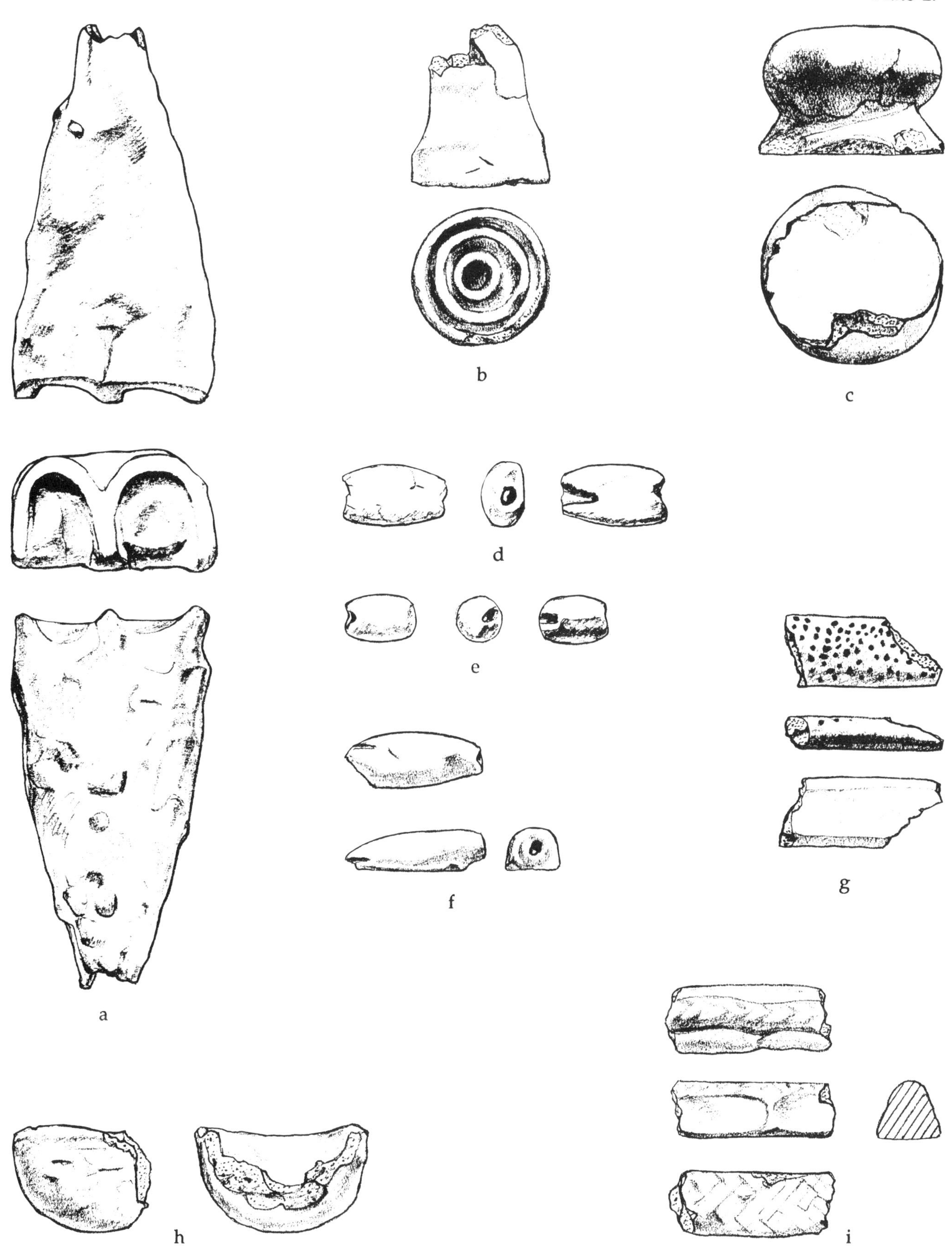

Çayönü—Geometric, Miscellaneous, and Non-Classifiable Fragment Forms: (*a*, *b*) Miscellaneous Stamp Seals, (*c*) Miscellaneous Smoother, (*d-f*) Miscellaneous Beads, (*g*) Geometric Pellet-Shaped Object, (*h*) Miscellaneous Miniature Vessel, and (*i*) Non-Classifiable Triangular-Shaped Rod.
Scale 1:1.

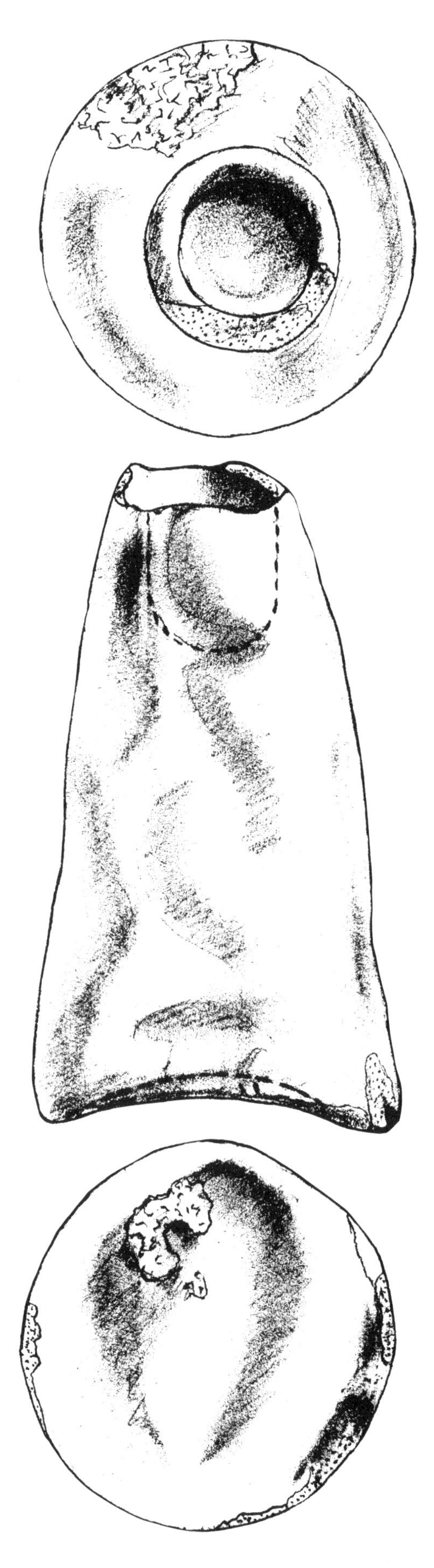

Çayönü—Miscellaneous Form: Pestle-Shaped Object. Scale 1:1.

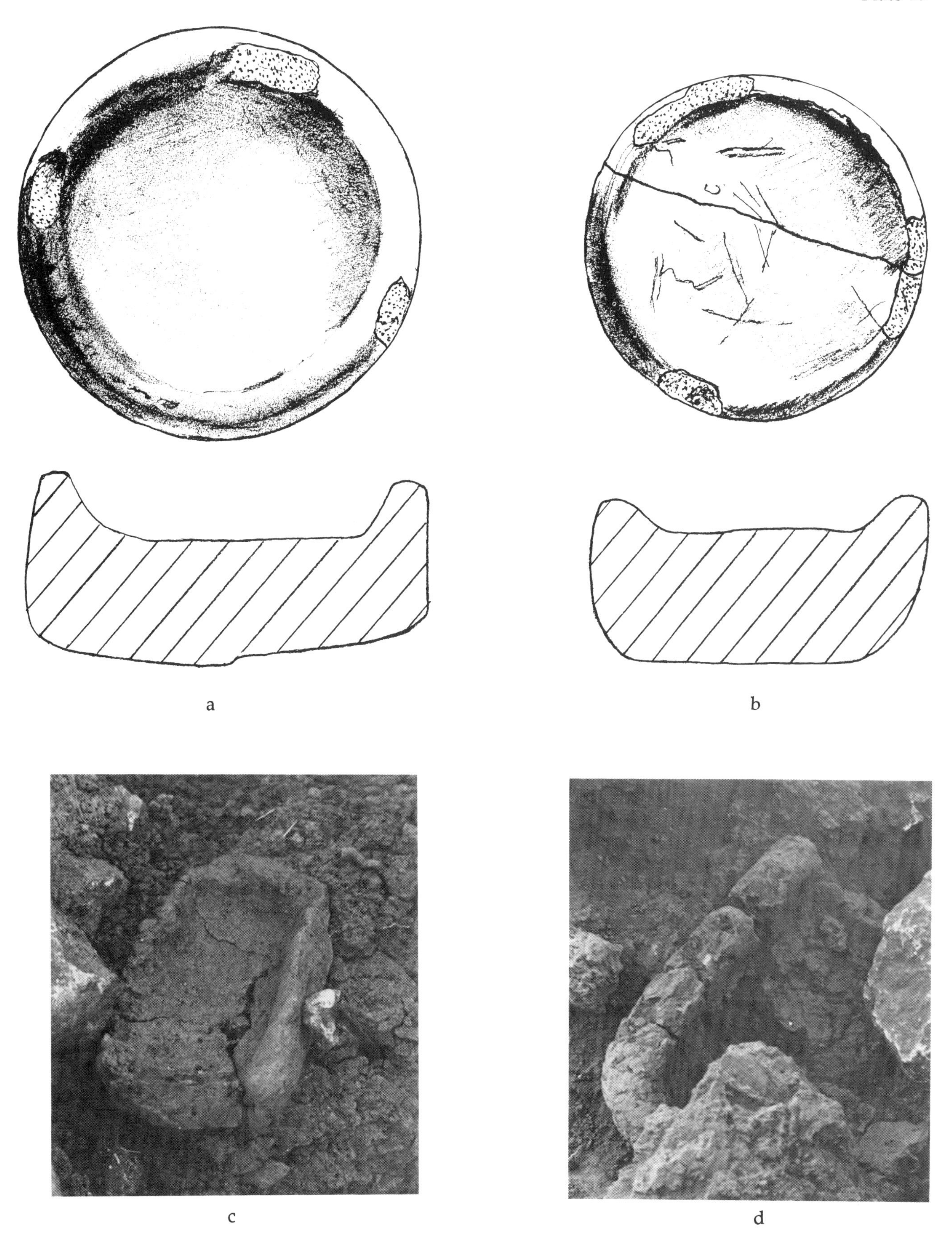

Çayönü—Miscellaneous Form: (*a, b*) Shallow Basins, (*c*) Shallow Basin in situ, and (*d*) Shallow "Basin-Like" Object with One End Open, in situ. Scale *a, b* 1:2, and *c, d* 1:5 (approx.).

Çayönü—Miscellaneous Form: Reconstructed House Model (*a*, front view and *b*, side view). Scale 1:1.

GENERAL BIBLIOGRAPHY

Adams, Robert McC.

1983 "The Jarmo Stone and Pottery Vessels Industries," in Linda S. Braidwood et al., eds., *Prehistoric Archeology Along the Zagros Flanks*. Oriental Institute Publications 105:209-32. Chicago: The Oriental Institute of The University of Chicago.

Bökönyi, Sándor

1977 *The Animal Remains from Four Sites in the Kermanshah Valley, Iran: Asiab, Sarab, Dehsavar, and Siabid.* British Archaeological Reports, Supplementary Series, vol. 34. Oxford: British Archaeological Reports.

Braidwood, Linda S.; Braidwood, Robert J.; Howe, Bruce; Reed, Charles A.; and Watson, Patty Jo

1983 *Prehistoric Archeology Along the Zagros Flanks.* Oriental Institute Publications 105. Chicago: The Oriental Institute of The University of Chicago.

Braidwood, Robert J.

1960a "Preliminary Investigations Concerning the Origins of Food-Production in Iranian Kurdistan," *British Association for the Advancement of Science* 17:214-18.

1960b "Seeking the World's First Farmers in Persian Kurdistan," *Illustrated London News* 237: 695-97.

1961 "The Iranian Prehistoric Project," *Iranica Antiqua* 1:3-7.

1968 "First Steps Toward a Food-Producing Way of Life in Late Prehistoric Iran," *Archaeologia Viva* 1:15-17.

1972 "Prehistoric Investigations in Southwestern Asia," *Proceedings of the American Philosophical Society* 116:310-20.

1986 "The Origin and Growth of a Research Focus—Agricultural Beginnings," *Expedition* 28 (no. 2):2-7.

Braidwood, Robert J., Howe, Bruce, and Reed, Charles A.

1961 "The Iranian Prehistoric Project," *Science* 133:2008-10.

Broman Morales, Vivian

1983 "Jarmo Figurines and Other Clay Objects," in Linda S. Braidwood et al., eds., *Prehistoric Archeology Along the Zagros Flanks.* Oriental Institute Publications 105:369-426. Chicago: The Oriental Institute of The University of Chicago.

Çambel, Halet and Braidwood, Robert J.

1980 "The Joint Istanbul-Chicago Universities' Prehistoric Research Project in Southeastern Anatolia. Comprehensive View: the Work to Date, 1963-1972," in Halet Çambel and Robert J. Braidwood, eds., *Prehistoric Research in Southeastern Anatolia* 1:33-64. Istanbul: Edebiyat Facultesi Basimevi (Chicago: Oriental Institute Publications Office).

1983 "Çayönü Tepesi: Schritte zu neuen Lebensweisen," in R. M. Boehmer and H. Hauptmann, eds., *Beiträge zur Altertumskunde Kleinasiens*, pp. 155-66. Mainz: von Zabern.

Flannery, Kent V.

1983 "Early Pig Domestication in the Fertile Crescent: a Retrospective Look," in Young, T. Cuyler, Jr.; Smith, Philip E. L.; and Mortensen, Peder, eds., *The Hilly Flanks and Beyond.* Studies in Ancient Oriental Civilization 36:163-88. Chicago: The Oriental Institute of The University of Chicago.

Henricksen, Elizabeth F. and McDonald, Mary F. A.

1983 "Ceramic Form and Function: an Ethnographic Search and an Archeological Application," *American Anthropologist* 85:630-45.

Hole, Frank

1977 *Studies in the Archeological History of the Deh Luran Plain.* Memoirs of the Museum of Anthropology 9. Ann Arbor: University of Michigan.

1987 "Chronologies in the Iranian Neolithic," in O. Aurenche, J. Evin, and F. Hours, eds., *Chronologie du Proche Orient.* British Archaeological Reports, International Series 379 (1): 353-79. Oxford: British Archaeological Reports.

Hole, Frank, Flannery, Kent V., and Neely, James A.

1969 *Prehistory and Human Ecology of the Deh Luran Plain.* Memoirs of the Museum of Anthropology 9. Ann Arbor: University of Michigan.

Lawrence, Barbara

1980 "Evidences of Animal Domestication at Çayönü," in Halet Çambel and Robert J. Braidwood, eds., *Prehistoric Research in South-Eastern Anatolia*. 1:285-308. Istanbul: Edebiyat Facultesi Basimevi (Chicago: Oriental Institute Publications Office).

1982 "Principal Food Animals at Çayönü," in Linda S. and Robert J. Braidwood, eds., *Prehistoric Village Archaeology in Southeastern Turkey*. British Archaeological Reports, International Series 138:175-99. Oxford: British Archaeological Reports.

Lawrence, Barbara and Reed, Charles A.

1983 "The Dogs of Jarmo," in Linda S. Braidwood et al., eds., *Prehistoric Archeology Along the Zagros Flanks*. Oriental Institute Publications 105:485-94. Chicago: The Oriental Institute of The University of Chicago.

Levine, Louis D.

1976 "The Mahidasht Project," *Iran* 14:160.

Levine, Louis D. and McDonald, Mary M. A.

1977 "The Neolithic and Chalcolithic Periods in the Mahidasht," *Iran* 15:39-50.

McDonald, Mary M. A.

1979 *An Examination of Mid-Holocene Settlement Patterns in the Central Zagros Region of Western Iran*. Ph. D. dissertation, Department of Anthropology, University of Toronto.

Mortensen, Peder

1964 "Early Village Farming Occupation," in J. Meldgaard, P. Mortensen, and H. Thrane, "Excavations at Tepe Guran, Luristan," *Acta Archaeologica* 34:97-133.

Özbek, Metin

1988 "Culte des Crânes humains à Çayönü," *Anatolica* 15:127-37.

Schaller, George B.

1980 *Stones of Silence, Journeys in the Himalaya*. New York: Viking Press.

Schirmer, Wulf

1983 "Drei Bauten des Çayönü Tepesi," in R. M. Boehmer and H. Hauptmann, eds., *Beitrage zur Altertumskunde Kleinasiens*, pp. 463-75. Mainz: von Zabern.

1988 "Zu den Bauten des Çayönü Tepesi," *Anatolica* 15:139-59.

Stech, T.

in press "Early Copper Metallurgy in Southwestern Asia," *Archeomaterials* 4.1.